Patterson Fire Department Centennial Book

And History of the Department
Patterson, N.Y.

1921-2021

Written & Complied By
Larry A. Maxwell

This Book is Dedicated To
All the Members of the Patterson Fire Department
Who Faithfully Served This Department
and
To Their Families Who Sacrificed So Much
To Let Them Serve With Us

Cover Design by Matthew Reid Maxwell

ISBN: 978-1-949277-12-8

© COPYRIGHT 2021 – LARRY A. MAXWELL – All Rights Reserved by Patterson Fire Dept.

Centennial Committee

Andrew Aiken, Susan Goldsmith, Loretta Kennedy. John Deitz, Mario Gabrielli, Debbie Miller, Larry Mendel, Larry Maxwell

Acknowledgements & Special Thanks

Special Thanks to Former Chief & Former President Robert Bell and to Associate Member Susan Goldsmith Who Served on the Centennial Book Committee.

Some of the pictures in this book were found in the archives of the Patterson Fire Department. A few came from the Putnam County Historian's Office and the Patterson Historical Society, many were submitted by members or friends of the department.

All photographs are presented without attribution.

Some photographs are of low quality but were used for unique content.

We are thankful for pictures provided. Special thanks to everyone who provided images for this book, that included Andrew Aiken, Robert Bell, John Bodor, Ed Centofante, John Deitz, May Ludington, Angie McGoorty, Trudy Mill, Kathy Petty, Andrew Rossi, Bob Smith Sr., Adam Stiebeling, and Others.

Special thanks to Ed O'Connell for the use of his mother Mary O'Connell's photo albums and for the many pictures from those albums used in this book.
Special thanks also to John Simpson for taking pictures of our current companies and for providing many other high quality pictures.

Special thanks to those who helped spend hours identifying people in photographs and providing information, that included: The Women's Auxiliary of the Patterson Fire Department and past chiefs Bob Bell Jr., Willie Boone, John "Snooky" Covell,
Bob Smith Sr., Caleb Franklin Smith III, Adam Stiebeling, James Tence and Ed O'Connell and past president Henry Brunow

Table of Contents

Introduction	7
History of the Patterson Fire Department	9
Our Buildings	43
Our Firefighting Vehicles Over the Years	50
Our Equipment & Turn Out Gear	63
Our Fire Police	70
Our Rescue & Ambulance Squad	73
Patterson Fire Department Women's Auxiliary	77
Organizations Within the Department	81
Putnam Lake Fire Department	83
Our Members Training	84
Our Department on Fire & Rescue Calls	95
Our Members in Parades	117
Activities With Our Department	125
Our Members Over the Years	138
Current Officers	185
Current Companies	186
Current Women's Auxiliary	190
Current Associate Members	190
Our Presidents	191
Our Chiefs	194
Our Chaplains	199
Members Who Served in the Military	201
Current Members	202
Memorials	203
Sponsors & Well-Wishers	206
Boosters	213
Remembering Departed Members	214
About the Author	216

Introduction

This book was put together as a labor of love, without compensation, for the centennial celebration of the Patterson Fire Department, in Patterson, New York. It is designed to present an authoritative, well-researched history of the department and to serve as a historical scrapbook featuring pictures of people, apparatus, and events.

The Patterson Fire Department is incorporated in the state of New York as Patterson Fire Department No. 1, Inc. It is a volunteer membership organization. It operates with authority from the Town of Patterson and the State of New York. Its members are primarily residents from the Town of Patterson, New York.

Photographs for this book were collected from various sources. Many photographs owned by the department were destroyed when the basement of the firehouse flooded. We are grateful to those who provided images. The sad thing is almost all the pictures provided did not identify the people in them, nor the dates the photos were taken. We are extremely grateful to those who helped identify people in the pictures. We are sorry we were not able to identify everyone. No young children are identified by name in this book without proper permission. We apologize for misidentified people or misspelled names.

We are also thankful to those who helped make it possible for us to make this book available to others by donating financially as Boosters or by sponsoring a Memorial or Well Wish in the back of this book.

Postcard of Patterson Railroad Avenue Ca. 1917 Now Front Street

Much of the detailed information presented in this book was derived from a careful review of the written minutes from the business meetings of the Patterson Fire Department. The minute books were missing for a few years. The minute books from 1921 through 1960 and the one from 1970 through 1980 were discovered. The minute book for 1960 through 1970 was missing. In 1980 the department purchased a cassette tape recorder and started to record the meetings. Few written minutes were kept after that date and made research for this book more difficult.

Back in 1921, when the Patterson Fire Department was organized, the center of town was located near the site of the current railroad station. Back then that was an industrial center with some factories and stores. The rest of the town was rural and included a number of dairy farms. The population of the town was about 1,230 people.

In 1921, the automobile was fairly new on the scene, but its popularity grew rapidly. Only four roads in town were paved. Those roads were later called Route 311, Route 22, Route 292, and Fair Street. Many of the other roads were impassable when it rained or snowed. Logs were placed on muddy sections of other roads to make them more passable.

Gas lights started to appear in Patterson in 1899. They remained popular for many years but became the source of numerous accidental fires. In 1902, the first phone lines appeared in town, but phones were considered a novelty until after the fire department started in 1921. Phones did not become a fixture in many homes until the 1950's. In April 1921, the same month the Patterson Fire Department was formed, high power electric lines first reached the town.

In 2021, one hundred years after the Patterson Fire Department was formed, the town is quite different from the way it was in 1921. The population is almost ten times greater. The industrial part, which was in the center of town, as well as the dairy farms, are gone. The town still retains some rural character but has become mainly a *bedroom community* because the majority of its residents commute to work in New York City and other areas. Those changes are a major factor making it more difficult for organizations in Patterson, like the fire department, to find volunteers.

The Patterson Fire Department is still a volunteer organization and is grateful to each member who makes the personal sacrifice to serve our community as part of our department and to their families who let them serve. We are always looking for more people who want to join us to help protect our community.

History of the Patterson Fire Department

By Dr. Larry A. Maxwell

This section started by using material gleaned from the brief historical summaries written for previous anniversary booklets by Robert Bell, John Bodor, and S. Delvalle Goldsmith. Information was also used from the Historic Patterson section listed on the Town of Patterson's website. That inspired hundreds of hours of in-depth research of department minutes, files, newspaper articles, and an in-depth review of federal, state, county and local records, along with interviews with numerous people.

To better understand the Patterson Fire Department, and its place in history, it is helpful to know some historical background of the Town of Patterson, New York. The area we now know as Patterson, New York was settled in the 1700's by Dutch and English immigrants, who leased land from the local Wappinger tribe.

From 1756 to 1763, ancestors of some of the founders of the Patterson Fire Department, along with members of the Wappinger Tribe, left their homes and families and went to fight in the French and Indian War. While they were gone, English landlord Beverly Robinson, who married into the wealthy Philipse family, produced some questionable, never before seen deeds, and claimed ownership of all the land in what would later be known as Patterson, New York. Robinson, with the backing of his friend, Sir Henry Moore, the Colonial Governor, then forced people to pay rent to him and evicted those who would not.

When Chief Daniel Nimham of the Wappinger Tribe returned from helping in the French and Indian War, he learned of Robinson's ploy. He hired an attorney and challenged Robinson's claims in court. Governor Moore arrested Nimham's attorney, Samuel Munrow. He then ruled in Robinson's favor. Munrow was an ancestor of this author (who is a member of the Pattterson Fire Department). Nimham appealed to King George and went to England to present his case. The Wappinger's claims were validated in England, yet Governor Moore refused to acknowledge them.

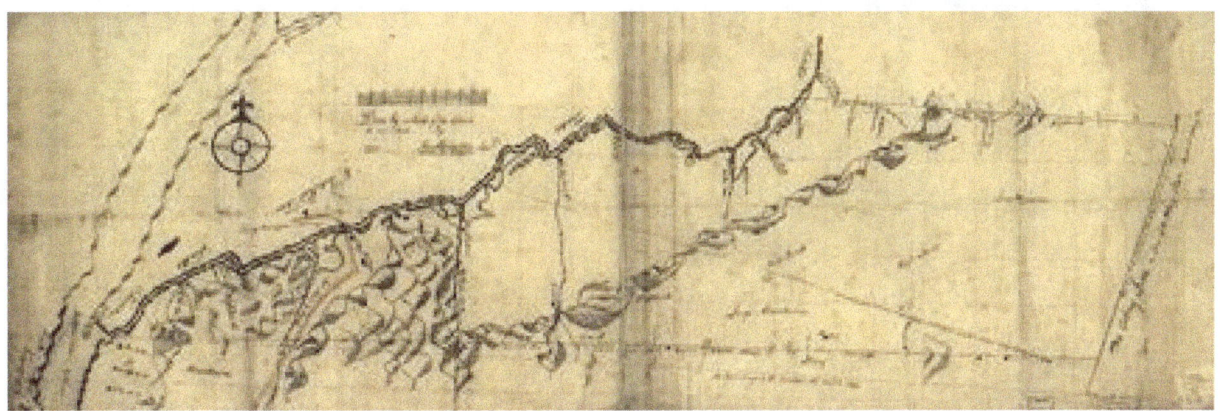

Colonial Map Showing the Disputed Lands

At the same time as Nimham was fighting his case in court, some 300 local settlers, including some who were ancestors of some of the founding members of the Patterson Fire Department, gathered near the current site of the Patterson Baptist Church in November 1765 and refused to pay rent to Robinson. Governor Moore responded and provided aide to his friend Beverly Robinson. He sent four regiments of British Regulars, along with a cannon crew, to put down the rebellion. In July of 1766, those British regulars faced off against Americans, on the land which would later become home to the Patterson Fire Department. A battle took place and the Regulars shot and killed Americans for the first time. That happened four years before the infamous Boston Massacre. That *Settler's Revolt*, as it became known, became the prelude to the American Revolution. Reports of the Settler's Revolt appeared in Boston newspapers and inspired Samuel Adams to write, *"It is time for the Sons of Liberty to unite!"*

When the Revolutionary War started in 1775, Beverly Robinson formed the first regiment of Loyalists to fight on the side of the Crown against local people. Henry Ludington, who was a colonel in the local militia, renounced his loyalty to the Crown and became Colonel of the 7th Regiment of the Dutchess County Militia (Patterson was part of Dutchess County back then). In 1777, Colonel Ludington's sixteen year old daughter Sybil Ludington became America's first female teenage military heroine. She made her famous 40 mile nighttime ride to call out the militia to stop an attack by Crown Forces. That attack was a key element in the Crown Forces plan to end the Revolution. Because of the efforts of Sybil, her father, along with ancestors of some of the founders of the Patterson Fire Department, the Crown Forces plan was defeated, the Revolution continued, and our Liberty was secured.

One hundred and forty-four years later, in 1921, Daniel G. Ludington, a relative of Colonel Henry and Sybil Ludington, became one of the founding members of the Patterson Fire Department. Then in 1922, his father, Henry S. Ludington, Postmaster for the Town of Patterson, became a Captain in the fire department and then the department's first Chief.

Sybil Ludington in 1777

Henry S. Ludington

Before the Revolutionary War, Patterson was called Fredericksburg. It was part of Dutchess County (In 1812, Putnam County was formed from the lower part of Dutchess County). Atter the war, the town was renamed Franklin in honor of Benjamin Franklin. At that time, other towns in New York also adopted the name Franklin. The town had to find a new name. In 1808, the town was renamed as the Town of Patterson. It was named after Scottish immigrant and Revolutionary War hero Matthew Patterson. Some early historians misunderstood his handwriting and spelled the name Paterson with one t. Original documents show Matthew Patterson clearly signed his name with two t's. The City of Paterson, New Jersey was named after William Paterson, the Governor of New Jersey, who spelled his name with one t. Despite the difference in the two town's spelling, people often mistake the one town for the other.

Until 1921, there was no official fire department in the Town of Patterson. When there was a fire, local residents rallied together and formed bucket brigades to try to put out the fires. They often used water brought to the scene in milk tanks transported on horse drawn wagons. They also extended a call for help to neighboring towns with existing fire departments. The towns of Brewster (1870), Pawling (1895), and Carmel (1915), all had fire departments which were called upon at different times. On at least one occasion the Brewster Fire Department responded by sending firefighting equipment to Patterson on a train. The lack of water close to fires, and the distance of the other departments who tried to help, often resulted in catastrophic loss.

Bucket Brigade

In December 1918, local business owners: Jacob Bloch (spelling later changed to Block), John E. Carey, and Mortimer B. Townsend, began an effort to raise money to buy two chemical trucks and a hook and ladder truck to provide fire protection in town. They raised enough money to purchase an old chemical truck.

Chemical trucks were not like most modern firefighting apparatus. They did not use plain water. They worked on the same principle as the soda-acid fire extinguisher in use at that time. Those trucks had tanks mounted on a chassis. Those tanks were filled with bicarbonate soda water. When there was a fire, sulfuric acid was added to the tanks. That caused a chemical reaction which created pressure and forced the solution through a hose. That provided enough pressure to reach the fourth floor of a building.

In early 1921, after the first chemical truck was acquired, Bloch, Carey, and Townsend, took the next steps necessary to form a fire department. They were joined by David Coleman Nichols, and other residents of Patterson. They started a petition drive and gathered enough signatures to petition the *Putnam County Board of Supervisors* to form a Fire District in Patterson. The law in New York State requires fire departments must be formed with the approval of a municipality. Once formed, those fire departments then answer to their municipality.

On April 7, 1921, David Nichols appeared before the Patterson Town Board and requested approval to form a volunteer fire department. At that time, the Town Board consisted of George F. Jennings, John Franklin Smith, Ward Segur, Junia W. Dykeman, Jr., David V. Smith, and William O. Taylor. The Board approved Nichol's request and the Patterson Fire Department was officially established by a resolution of the Town Board. The minutes of that town board meeting read as follows (birth year of the members were not in the resolution but are added to provide a better picture of the people involved):

> Mr. D. C. Nichols appeared before the Board in regard to the establishment of a Fire Department and reported the information obtained as to the procedure necessary. Motion was made and seconded that the following named persons be appointed as members of the Town Fire Department. Forty-two men.

Ernest Anderson (1893)	D.C. Nichols (1848)
Hjalma Anderson* (1896)	Ralph C. Nichols (1887)
James Bennett (1862)	Frank Osborne (1883)
Jacob Bloch (Block) (1896)	Louis G. Pendleton* (1895)
Michael Burns (1897)	George Pfahl (1875)
George Burton (1889)	George Robinson (1886)
John E. Carey (1870)	Ward Rogers (1899)
Elbert Crosby (1875)	Andrew Rutledge (1876)
Abel Davis (1893)	William Rutledge (1874)
Junia W. Dykeman (1879)	Ward Segur (1885)
Gordon Eastwood*(1893)	Theron Smalley (1886)
John F. Eastwood* (1887)	Clarence Smith* (1892)
Vincent Gaydos (1890)	David V. Smith (1874)
Dr. Reed F. Haviland (1869)	Daniel Steinbeck (1883)
Alfred Hawley (1873)	Ernest Tompkins (1881)
Frank E. Hayt (1896)	Dr. Albert N. Towner* (1886)
Bert Hiser (1888)	Mortimer B. Townsend (1862)

Howard Kelley* (1899)	Paul Townsend* (1895)
Douglas Kent (1861)	Rev. H. F. Watts* (1886)
Howard Knapp* (1898)	George Witheridge (1872)
Daniel Ludington (1887)	Samuel Woods (1892)

*An * after name indicates person was World War I Veteran*

All but five of the original 42 members of the fire department were born in New York. George Burton was born in South Dakota and Rev. Henry H. Watts was born in Kansas.

Since its beginning, the department has always included immigrants. Of the founding members: David V. Smith (who later became a president of the department) was born in Canada; Hjalmar Anderson was born in Sweden; and Vincent Gaydos was born in the Austro-Hungarian Empire in Europe, in an area which would later be called Czechoslovakia, then Slovokia.

The youngest member of the department was Howard Kelley. He was 21 years old and a veteran of World War One. At that time 21 was the youngest age allowed for firemen in New York. The oldest member was David Coleman Nichols. He was 73 years old. He died in 1930 from a heart attack after his barn caught fire.

The original members had a variety of occupations. Twelve worked on farms. Dr. Albert N. Towner was a Veterinarian. Dr. Reed Ferris Haviland was a medical doctor. James A. Bennett was an attorney. Rev. Henry F. Watts was Pastor of the Presbyterian Church. Mortimer B. Townsend owned the sash factory in town. His son Paul was bookkeeper for the company and also a member. Vincent Gaydos owned a department store. John E. Carey and George Pfahl owned grocery stores. Andrew Rutledge was a mail carrier. Ernest Tompkins was a machinist. Louis Pendleton was a clerk for the new electric company. Michael Burns and Abel Davis were drivers (Those two were called chauffeurs on the census. That was a very new occupation at that time). Frank Hayt (also spelled Hyat) and Douglas Kent were listed on the census as having no occupation. Hayt later became Clerk to the Putnam County Board of Supervisors.

Two of the original members: Junia Dykeman and Ward Segur served on the Town Board, which approved formation of the department. All the members lived in the Town of Patterson except Abel Davis. He was born in Holmes but lived on the border in Brewster. Nine members were veterans of World War I. Dr. Albert Towner served as a Major in the United States Army.

One hundred years later, in 2021, the department has 64 listed active members. The oldest member, Edward Centofante, is a 96 year old World War II veteran. He still responds to calls. Nine members are women. Most of the members were born in New York State. Four were born in other countries, including: Guatemala, Ecuador, Peru, and Romania. Current members have a variety of occupations including: construction workers, electricians, artisans, business owners, computer professionals, military, professional fire fighters, law enforcement officers, medics, and an ordained minister.

After the formation of the department was authorized by the town the first official meeting of the Patterson Fire Department was held on April 26, 1921, in the Town Clerk's office in Stahl's Hall. The following is the record of the meeting filed by Fire Department Clerk, L. G. Pendleton:

> The first regular meeting of the Patterson Fire Department was held in the Town Clerk's office on the above date. Meeting called to order by D. C. Nichols. On motion D. C. Nichols was elected Chairman of the meeting. Chairman called for nominations for Captain. Dr. R. F. Haviland was nominated and duly elected. Chairman called for nominations for Clerk. W. P. Townsend and L. G. Pendleton were nominated. D. D. Kent and H. E. Kelley were appointed tellers. There were 21 votes cast. P. W. Townsend received 11 and L. G. Pendleton received 10. Mr. Townsend refused the office because he had so many other duties of the same nature and made a motion that one ballot be cast for L. G. Pendleton, motion seconded and carried L. G. Pendleton elected Clerk. Captain Haviland appointed the following committee to draw up By-laws and Regulations and report at the next meeting, H. E. Kelley, George Burton, and Dr. A. N. Towner. The next meeting was ordered for Tuesday evening May 3rd at 7 o'clock. There being no further business motion made and carried meeting adjourned.

At a meeting of the Patterson Town Board on May 23, 1921, they approved holding a special election on June 15, 1921 to raise $4,000 to be used for the purchase of apparatus and for other expenses to maintain and operate the new fire company. The referendum passed.

Our New 1921 Chemical Truck
In a Parade Down Main Street (Route 311).

After the department was formed in April 1921, it held a department meeting every month. The department held its second meeting on May 23, 1921, the same day the town met to approve the vote on funding for the department. At that department meeting, approval was given to repair a wheel on the chemical truck the department had at that time. They also approved paying for a handle to be welded on that same truck.

At the August 1, 1921 monthly meeting of the department, a resolution was approved asking the town to use the money it raised to buy a Buffalo Chemical Fire Apparatus to be mounted on an Oldsmobile chassis. That was produced by *Obenchain-Boyer* of Logansport, Indiana. The price was $3,500. It featured electric headlights, as well as a search light on the dashboard. It included 300 feet of hose, two half-gallon portable fire extinguishers, a 24 foot extension ladder, and a 12 foot ladder with hooks. It was able to reach a speed of up to 40 miles per hour. It was painted Sagamore Red with gold leaf, black stripes, trimming and lettering which read "Patterson Fire Dept. No 1."

Delivery of the new chemical truck was made on November 3, 1921. On Friday, November 4, 1921, the day after the fire truck arrived, the firemen put the new truck to the test. They set fire to some oil barrels. They used the new truck and effectively extinguished the fire. Three days later, at the November 7, 1921 meeting of the department, it requested the town provide them two 40' extension ladders, one dozen fire pails, and one 35'x5' fire and tube.

Pendleton & Townsend Sash & Blind Factory
Our first apparatus was housed for a few years in the boiler annex of this building.

When the department started, it did not have any buildings where its apparatus could be kept. At the May 21, 1921 meeting of the department, Mr. Peter O'Hara offered the department use of an old barn for $500 a month for five years. The barn needed repairs. They agreed to sign a lease if he repaired the barn. Instead, Mortimer Townsend, a member of the department and owner of the *Pendleton & Townsend Sash & Blind Factory*, allowed the department to store its apparatus, at no cost, in the boiler annex at his factory. That building was near where the current Town Recreation Building is located, on what is now called Front Street. That became home to the department's apparatus until 1928.

The first official fire call, after the new chemical truck was received, took place at 3:43 AM on December 29, 1921, at Ballard's Place. The log indicates the structure was a total loss.

Since 1921, the Patterson Fire Department has provided fire protection throughout our town, as well as assistance to departments in the surrounding area. In November of 1924, the department helped fight its first major forest fire in nearby Whaley Lake.

When the department started, it was headed by a Captain, who was assisted by a Lieutenant. They were aided in business matters by a paid Treasurer and paid Secretary.

On April 26, 1921, Dr. Reed F. Haviland (b. 1871) was elected the first Captain. He was a physician in Pawling and Patterson. He only served a few months and resigned. He was replaced on September 7, 1921 by Mortimer B. Townsend (b. 1862). He was one of the men who worked to get the fire department established. He also only served a few months. He was replaced at the annual meeting on May 1, 1922 by Henry S. Ludington (b. 1863). He was the town's Postmaster. He was the father of Daniel G. Ludington (one of the founding members) and relative of the local Revolutionary War heroes: Col. Henry Ludington and his daughter Sybil Ludington (who was known as the Female Paul Revere). Henry Ludington served as Captain for eight years.

At the annual meeting on May 5, 1930, the office of Captain was renamed Chief. Henry Ludington was elected and served as Chief until the next annual meeting in May 1931, when Junia W. Dykeman, Jr. (b. 1879) was elected Chief.

The Putnam House

Since the Patterson Fire Department started, fund raising has always been an important aspect of department life. Over the years, numerous methods were used. During its first month the department purchased a moving picture machine for $400 to show movies to raise money. The movies were shown in The *Putnam House* on Main Street (Route 311,) near Orchard Street, until the building was destroyed by a fire in 1928. The movies were then shown in other locations, including the Grange Hall.

On at least two occasions the department was given a calf to sell. The department also raised funds with dinners, turkey shoots, dances, and Bingo.

Starting in 1922, a new car was raffled off, almost every year. The first car raffled was a 1922 Star Car (pictured left).

In July 1930, the department raffled off a Marmon-Roosevelt Straight Eight car (pictured right). It was a larger luxurious, four door automobile.

Since its inception, the Patterson Fire Department developed a camaraderie with other fire departments. On September 4, 1922, the department participated in a parade and fireman's carnival in Carmel, New York. The department was awarded first place for the Most Popular Fire Department.

It helps to understand how world and national events had an effect on the Patterson Fire Department. The department was formed just after the end of what was called, *The War to End All Wars* (later called World War I). A number of the founding members fought in that war. After the war, the economy was booming and brought prosperity to many. A spirit of celebration swept across America. That brought about dramatic social changes. Nightclubs and dance halls sprung up all around the country. Along with that, the consumption of alcohol rose dramatically and reportedly had devastating effects on families. On January 19, 1919, two years before the Patterson Fire Department was officially organized, the United States Congress responded to the devastation cause by alcohol abuse and enacted the 18th Amendment. It prohibited the manufacture and sale of intoxicating liquors. The period known as *Prohibition* went into effect in January 1920. That amendment did not forbid the consumption of alcohol yet by forbidding its sale, that had a big effect on nightclubs and dance halls. Many closed. Some of them moved to secret locations and still served alcohol provided by organized crime.

During Prohibition, people still wanted to celebrate and dance. The 1920's became known as *The Roaring Twenties*. That celebratory attitude continued for many years. Some saw economic opportunity and formed troupes which travelled from town to town holding dances. They charged entrance fees and made a significant amount of money. During that period, the Patterson Fire Department saw the profitability of holding dances to raise funds and began to hold numerous dances throughout the year. It took a while before the traveling dance troupes reached Patterson. They became competition to the department's dances and a hurt fund raising efforts.

The department found a creative way to eliminate their competition. A number of serious fires occurred at some dances around the nation, so fire protection was required to hold a dance in many municipalities. At the January 7, 1929 meeting of the department, they helped put a stop to those other dances in town by passing a resolution which stated, *"No fire protection would be provided on occasions of second class dances by non-residents, as firemen refused to be on duty for such occasions."*

Though dances were profitable, the method which often raised the most funds for the department was the annual carnival. Carnivals were held every year starting in August of 1926. They were put on hold a few times during the Great Economic Depression of the 1930's and again during World War II. The first carnival earned $476. That may not sound like much money, but it must be remembered the average wage for workers in New York at that time was about $2 to $3 per day. The funds raised from that first carnival, along with other funds, enabled the department to purchase another fire fighting vehicle.

The department determined it needed to get a pumper truck, which used regular water to fight fires. By the end of 1926, fund raising efforts were successful and the department had enough money to buy the new piece of apparatus. At the December 6, 1926 meeting of the department, a representative of the *Hahn Motor Company* came and made a presentation explaining how its pumper truck worked. A special meeting was held on December 17, 1926. The department voted to approve the purchase of the new pumper if the town would purchase 150' of hose and furnish them a building to keep the new vehicle in.

In February of 1927, Mr. Cecil Barclay, representing the *Hahn Motor Company*, wrote the order for a Hahn 400 gallon pumper at a cost of $5,800. In appreciation of the order, he presented the department with a gift of six fire coats. Fire coats back then were basically rubber rain coats with metal latches. They provided little protection but did help. It was not uncommon for the firemen to wear blankets to protect themselves while fighting fires.

Delivery of the new Hahn pumper was delayed by a common mistake, that still occurs today. It was delivered to Paterson, New Jersey. After it made it up to Patterson, New York, the Hahn was in service for only a short time before an axle broke. That happened as it crossed the railroad tracks, while responding to a fire. The truck was overloaded with firefighters and members of the community who jumped on the truck to go to the fire. The truck had to be towed part of the way to the scene. Shortly thereafter the Chief issued an order that *"no civilians"* were to be permitted to ride the new fire truck to fires.

The first home to the Patterson Fire Department was *Stahl's Hall,* which was owned by Peter O'Hara. Stahl's Hall was located on Main Street (Route 311), near Locust Avenue. At that time, the first floor of the building served as the Town Hall. All meetings, and most activities of the department, were held in Stahl's Hall from its inception in 1921 until 1968 when Stahl's Hall was declared unsafe. In 1968, the department built its first building across the railroad tracks and Stahl's Hall was demolished. The hall contained a piano, which was used to provide entertainment as part of the regular monthly meetings. A committee was appointed to ensure there was entertainment at the meetings.

1912 Postcard of Stahl's Hall on Main Street.
The first floor of Stahl's Hall served as the Town Hall at that time.
Starting in 1921 the second floor of this building served as **Our First Home**.
A small garage, later built next to this building, provided to shelter our apparatus.

If one refers to the place where the fire apparatus is housed as *the firehouse* then the department's first firehouse was the boiler annex of the *Pendleton & Townsend Sash Company*. The department's first apparatus was housed there for its first seven years, from 1921 until 1927. That changed in 1928. In response to the departments resolution at the December 6, 1926 meeting, the Town of Patterson held a special meeting at the Patterson Town Hall on March 15, 1927. Voters approved $5,000 to buy hose and build a new garage for the Patterson Fire Department. It was stipulated the garage would belong to the town and also be used to store town machinery. The town used the funds to build a small garage next to the department's home in Stahl's Hall.

The new building was barely large enough to hold the department's equipment, so in February 1928, the town gave the department even greater use of Stahl's Hall. They authorized the department to remodel the second floor and to have exclusive use. The fire department added cabinets and decorated the place. During cold winter months they received permission to hold their meetings on the first floor in the Town Clerk's office which had heat. Later the department installed water and heat.

The department had a problem with people parking in front of the new garage. In February 1929, they painted the words, *Patterson Fire Company No. 1*, in gold letters on the garage. After the words were painted on the building, the February 22, 1929 issue of The Putnam County Courier reported, *there should be no excuse for anyone parking a car in front of the building or near enough to prevent the easy turning of the fire engine after leaving the building.*

Back in 1927 at the May 2nd meeting, the department made two special first time appointments. They appointed Jay Von Berg to serve as the town's first Fire Marshall and ordered a Fire Marshall badge. For many years it was the fire department which made that appointment.

At the same meeting, the department appointed Rev. Horace H. Hillery, Pastor of the Presbyterian Church, to be the department's first chaplain. Rev. Hillery joined the department in 1926. The department ordered a special badge for him. That meeting ended with a prayer by Chaplain Hillery. After that, all meetings were opened in prayer.

To fight fires effectively, fire departments divide their members into various *companies*, with different responsibilities. During its early years, the department companies were based on the equipment available at the time, rather than on vehicles. There first companies were: Company 1 - Ladders and Axes; Company 2 – Hose; and Company 3 - Buckets and Chemicals. Today, companies are assigned to vehicles, such as: Heavy Rescue, Ladder Truck, Engine, Tanker, Brush Truck, Ambulance, and Fire Police.

In August 1927, the department started to hold regular weekly drills. That is a practice which continues to the present day. It was only halted during the Corona Virus pandemic, when in March 2020, national and state shutdowns were imposed.

Fire departments are considered a para-military organization. Most fire departments have a designated uniform for its members. Those uniforms are only worn for special occasions such as: parades, funerals, and other formal occasions. The first mention of uniforms for the department was at a special meeting on August 24, 1927. It was decided to get a blue uniform coat with buttons. The department agreed to pay half the cost and each member would pay the other half.

Many are not aware that though fire departments help fight fires, that is only part of what they do. Another large part of their role is helping to rescue people, and even animals on some occasions. Specialized training is provided to members in firefighting and rescue.

On August 6, 1928, a representative of the *Mine Safety Apparatus Company* from Pittsburg, Pennsylvania came to Patterson and showed members of the department how to use safety appliances and a first aid kit. He also demonstrated a newly refined medical rescue procedure called *artificial respiration*. That equipment became part of the department's ever expanding tools.

The October 28, 1928 issue of the Pawling newspaper, reported proceeds from the October 31st Fireman's Dance at the Patterson Fire Department would be used to purchase an ambulance. Since those early years some type of ambulance service was provided. Twenty-one years later, at the June 3, 1949 meeting, the department agreed to cooperate with the Putnam Lake Fire Department on mutual aid for ambulance service.

Over the years the department added additional equipment to help fight fires and save lives. One common unexpected item was very useful. On April 9, 1930, the department authorized the purchase of four brooms for fighting grass fires. The department also used some uncommon items. On May 4, 1931, the department authorized purchasing gas masks.

As the number of fire calls increased, the department sought new apparatus to help expand its capabilities. At the October 21, 1929 meeting of the department, a resolution was made to purchase a supply truck to transport firemen to fires and to carry additional supplies. The motion was defeated. The motion was modified, submitted for a vote, and defeated again. It was then modified a third time and submitted for a vote. The last version approved buying a supply truck in the future when funds became available. Little did they realize the impending economic crisis which would soon strike.

Eight days after that meeting, on October 29, 1929, the stock market crashed. The next day there was a run on banks all across America. Banks ran out of money and closed their doors.

That brought on the *Great Depression*, which swept across America.

Shortly after the Great Depression started, things became even worse. Severe drought struck the Midwest and lasted almost a decade. The drought was felt as far east as New York. Many people lost their homes and jobs. *The Salvation Army* made appeals to raise funds to help people. The Patterson Fire Department replied by making a monthly donation. They also established their own fund to help local families in need. In addition, they also donated to

The American Red Cross Drought Relief Fund. Volunteer Fire Departments are governed by numerous laws in New York State. They are listed under the New York State Charities Law because they provide a service to members of the community at no cost to residents. That law allows the department to provide not only fire assistance but other relief to the community.

It is important to understand the Patterson Fire Department and the Putnam Lake Fire Department are staffed by volunteers and are guided by some different laws than the neighboring fire departments in Brewster, Carmel, and Pawling, which are also staffed by volunteers. An entirely different set of laws apply to municipalities with a paid fire department, such as Mount Vernon or New York City.

The Town of Patterson has two *Fire Protection Districts*. The Towns of Brewster, Carmel and Pawling are different. Those towns are designated as a *Fire District*. A *Fire District* has a *Board of Fire Commissioners* elected by the taxpayers. By state law, an election is held among residents, for the Fire Commissioners on the second Tuesday in December. Any fire department in such a town answers to the Board of Fire Commissioners. That board must approve all members and funding for the department. In a Fire District, the Fire Commissioners put together an annual detailed budget, which is included in the Town's Budget. The Town Board is not allowed to change that budget. That budget is not voted on, it is part of a direct tax levy to residents. The Fire Commissioners therefore receive their funding directly from the taxpayers, hence they operate directly with taxpayers dollars and must answer to the taxpayers for how they spend their money. Taxpayers can express approval or disapproval with the Fire Commissioners by electing them or different people.

Fire Departments in a town which have a designated *Fire Protection District*, like the Town of Patterson, operate differently than towns with a *Fire District*. In Patterson, the fire departments operate as an independent organization, guided by their constitution and by-laws and by their own members. As such, the Patterson Fire Department and the Putnam Lake Fire Departments are separate entities. They contract with the town to provide fire protection for their designated area for an agreed upon amount, just as any other contracted providers with the town. Unlike a town with a Fire District, where towns cannot modify the fire budget, in towns with a Fire Protection District, like Patterson, the towns can negotiate the amount requested by the fire department. The two parties come to a final agreed upon amount, just as with any other contract. Though the funds the town receives are from the taxpayers, when the department receives the funds they are not considered such, just as the funds received by any other contractor are not considered tax payer money.

In 1921, shortly after it was formed, the Patterson Fire Department considered asking the town to be redesignated as a Fire District but chose not to pursue that route.

Under the Patterson Fire Department's original Constitution and By-laws, business meetings were conducted under the leadership of the Captain. An organizational change was made and put into effect at the annual meeting on May 5, 1930. It was then the office of President of the fire department was established. Junia W. Dykeman, Jr. was elected as the department's first President. He was a member of the Town Board, a Trustee at the Patterson Baptist Church and founding member of the Patterson Fire Department. At that same meeting, the office of Trustee was also added. Three founding members of the department, were elected to serve as the first Trustees: John E. Carey; David V. Smith; and Mortimer B. Townsend. The office of Vice President was not added until decades later.

On June 2, 1930, the month after the organizational change, the department authorized changing the sign on the garage which housed the fire apparatus, from "Patterson Fire Company No. 1." to "Patterson Fire Dept."

At the September 8, 1930 meeting of the department, Mr. Jameson, from the *Hahn Motor Company*, made a presentation urging the department to purchase a Hahn Supply Tanker with a Booster Tank for $3,400. Jameson was an effective salesman. He convinced the department to pass a resolution to buy the truck and sign a contract at that meeting, even though the department did not have the money to pay for the tanker.

At the November 3, 1930 meeting, approval was granted to withdraw $800 from the account with the Pawling Savings Bank and to secure an $800 loan from the Pawling National Bank, to help pay for the Hahn Supply Tanker.

Though buying more effective fire equipment was a good thing, it appears the department gave some serious thought to whether it was really a good idea to spend money it did not have, especially during the difficult depression the country was dealing with. At the December 1, 1930 meeting, the department appointed a committee to consider cancelling the purchase. The committee reported back at the next meeting in January, that they were successful. The next fire truck was not acquired until 1932.

At that same December 1 meeting, it was agreed the department would start to undertake efforts to inform the public about *Fire Prevention Week*. That expanded over the years to include the department conducting special programs in and for the schools.

At a special meeting of the department on December 22, 1930, when the Great Depression was affecting people in Patterson, the department voted to set aside a fund to provide relief for any local residents who became destitute and needed assistance. On April 6, 1931, the department voted to expand its contributions to that relief fund.

Across the sea, the Great Depression gave rise to Adolf Hitler in Germany, Benito Mussolini in Italy, and Imperialism in Japan. Those three would eventually unite. That in turn lead to a World War which would have a direct impact on the Patterson Fire Department.

In the midst of those troubling world events, on January 12, 1933, the department voted to purchase its first property. It was the Sheffield Ice Company Pond. The department wanted

the pond (pictured here) for their exclusive use as a water source for fighting fires. The pond was next to the railroad tracks and Main St. (Route 311). It also included a ball field the department used for many activities.

Twenty-one years later, in 1954, the department bought three acres of land, next to the pond and ballfield, from Howard Burdick. Then, five years later, in 1959, Burdick did a wonderful thing, he gave the department an adjoining piece of land. The only thing the department had to do was pay for the cost to change the deed. Years later, in 1991, that land became the site of the present firehouse.

On March 6, 1933, the department voted to incorporate as a membership corporation. That did not make any significant change in offices or operation of the department. Eight months after that Congress passed the 21st Amendment repealling Prohibition.

For many years the department bought books of raffle tickets to help support other fire departments, just as those departments bought tickets from this department. In the Summer of 1933, the department bought some raffle tickets for a new car from the Dover Plains Fire Department. At the August 7, 1933 meeting of the department, it was recorded the department won a new two door Chevy Coach car. That car had a closed roof. They held a special meeting on August 14, 1933, and decided to try to trade that Chevy for a new *Master Six Chevy Touring Car*, which had an open roof. They said that would be better for the department to use as an emergency car. Over the next few months various car dealers were contacted in attempts to make a trade. The department was informed the Master Six Chevy, was no longer being manufactured. In June 1934, they sold the 1933 two door Chevy for $400. That was the retail price for a new version of that car.

1933 Chevy Coach

Chevy Master Six Touring Car

There are numerous bodies of water around the Town of Patterson. At the September 4, 1933 meeting, the department ordered a wooden boat be built to be used for water rescue. That boat never saw much use.

Sources of water to fight fires has always been an important need and concern in the town of Patterson. The town is not like many towns and cities which have pressurized fire hydrants, with a ready supply of water. Patterson depends on ponds and dry hydrants for its water to fight fires. Dry hydrants are situated next to water sources such as ponds. They extend down to the water source but do not have water pressure. A fire engine, pumper or tanker must hook a hose to the dry hydrant and use suction to draw out the water.

In November 1933, the town authorized the department to install its first dry hydrant on Front Street (shown here). That was to provide water from the Fireman's Pond, which was located across the railroad tracks The fire department purchased the supplies. The labor was provided by the *Work Relief Committee*, which used men unemployed due to the depression. A pipe was run under the railroad and a hydrant was installed. When the installation was completed they opened the hydrant to test it. When no water came out, some thought the hydrant did not work. They expected the hydrant to quickly disperse water with pressure. They did not understand it was a dry hydrant whose purpose is to provide easier access to the water in the pond. In the following years, additional dry hydrants were added and continue to be a main source for providing water to the fire apparatus.

Today, to prepare for calls, each vehicle stays filled with water. When it gets to a fire, the water in the apparatus is used to fight the fire. When the water is depleted it has to be refilled. It is either: refilled with a tanker; leaves the scene and goes to a water source to draw more water; or a portable water pond is set up (carried on some engines and pictured here). After a fire is extinguished, all vehicles are refilled with water.

At the February 5, 1934 meeting, the department minutes state a committee was appointed to look at building the department's first firehouse. Over the years various committees were formed but no action was taken on building a new firehouse until 1968.

One of the next vehicles the department acquired was a 1932 Dodge Fire Truck. It was a short vehicle used to transport men and equipment to fires. It became known as the *Squad Wagon*. It was a favorite in the department for many years.

Recreation and camaraderie plays a big part in the fire service. On December 5, 1935, the department approved looking into purchasing a pool table. On January 1. 1936, $200 was approved. That amount was enough to purchase a top of the line professional pool table. At the March 2, 1936 meeting it was reported they had the table. They appointed a committee to oversee its use. It became so popular people in town came to use the table, They had to restrict its use to members. Eventually, conflicts arose between some players and officers had to be present to oversee its use. In 1968, after the firehouse was built down the road, that pool table was moved to the new firehouse.

The Patterson Fire Department has always proved service to the schools in the community. Special programs were conducted in the schools. At the March 2, 1936 meeting, the department announced another service to the schools. If school was cancelled, the department would blast its fire siren three times at 7 am to inform the community of the school closing.

It is important to understand, fire equipment ages with use. At a special meeting on March 5, 1937, the department approved $6,000 to purchase a new pumper to replace the 1927 Hahn pumper. On March 29, 1937, they increased the amount to $6,500. Then on April 5, 1937, they authorized using those funds to purchase a 1937 Mack Pumper with a closed cab. The new truck was delivered in July.

On January 6, 1938 the department addressed another need. Fire departments usually provide a way to identify the personal vehicles their members drive. They authorized members to purchase bronze plaques to place on their own vehicles to identify themselves as members of the department.

In May 1939, New York State took legislative action which expanded the pool of volunteers for the fire service. The minimum age of active firefighters was lowered from 21 to 18.

Prior to 1939, the annual meeting of the department, and election of officers, was held in May each year. On January 9, 1939, the department voted to move the annual meeting and elections to April. Though the town later changed the department's fiscal year to a January to December basis, and though most departments around the state hold their annual meetings in December or January, the Patterson Fire Department still holds its annual meeting and elections in April each year.

The Town of Patterson has a distinct community known as Putnam Lake. Though some people lived in that area, the Putnam Lake Community did not come into existence until the 1930's. Real estate developers Warren and Arthur Smadbeck had an idea to develop a summer community in Putnam County. First, in 1928, they purchased land in Carmel. They constructed a dam and created Lake Carmel. Over the next decade more than 5,400 summer homes were built around that lake.

Three years later, in 1931, during the Great Depression, the Smadbeck Brothers, along with *The Daily Mirror*, a newspaper in New York City, seized on another opportunity. Land prices plummeted because of the Great Depression. They were optimistic and purchased five farms in Patterson, as well as some land in New Fairfield, Connecticut for a total of 1,111 acres. They erected a dam and created a 200 acre pond they called *Putnam Lake*. They mapped out 11,000 lots for cottages and businesses. They then marketed them to the public as a summer community. Even in the midst of the Great Depression, that first year they sold 75% of the lots. By 1944, 880 building were constructed. The Patterson Fire Department provided fire service to the new community.

1930's Postcard of the New Putnam Lake Community

In 1939, by the time the Great Depression was coming to an end, the population of Putnam Lake had grown significantly. That summer the Patterson Fire Department held its first carnival in Putnam Lake.

That same year the rapid military expansion of Germany and Japan caused great concern worldwide. On June 5, 1939, the department approved the purchase of a banner and flag with the name of the department. Concerns over the military expansion of the Imperial Japanese Empire was revealed at the July 17, 1939 meeting of the department. They approved buying a silk banner, staff, and strap, *provided it did not come from Japan.*

On a domestic note, at the September 4, 1939 meeting of the department, it approved purchasing new uniforms consisting of a red shirt, a belt, and white trousers. That was a significant change. Eight months later, at the May 6, 1940 meeting, people raised concerns over that uniform. The order for that uniform was rescinded. Instead they approved a uniform with blue trousers, white shirts, and black ties. It appears someone must have really liked red shirts because seven years later, at the January 2, 1947 meeting, they approved buying red satin shirts and blue trousers for their new uniform. Like the first time they were approved, people changed their minds. The following month, at the February 2, 1947 meeting, they rescinded that order.

The growth of Putnam Lake continued. At the September 2, 1940 meeting of the Patterson Fire Department, a representative of the *Putnam Lake Council* requested fire-fighting apparatus be kept at Putman Lake. It was not until the May 5, 1941 meeting of the department, that authorization was grated to keep an engine at Putnam Lake. The 1921 Chemical Truck began to be stationed there.

As military conflict spread world-wide, on October 7, 1940, the department passed a resolution stating, *Any and all men drafted into the army have a leave of absence from the company*. A similar resolution was reaffirmed again during the Korean War.

Posted Printed by The Putnam County Defense Council

Before America was directly involved in the war, on November 4, 1940, the department approved holding Bingo games to raise funds. At the January 6, 1941 meeting they announced they raised $150 from the first Bingo game. That was a considerable amount of money when you realize in 1940 the minimum wage was $0.30 per hour.

Bingo was a very profitable fund raising method used for many years. By the 1970's Bingo games were held every Wednesday night and generated a significant amount of funds. That continued until January of 1978, ten years after moving into the first new firehouse. At that time the room used for Bingo was divided into two rooms: a Recreation Room, and a Meeting Room. The Bingo supplies were sold to the Pawling Fire Department.

Eighty ago, at the February 4, 1941 meeting of the department, a radical new policy was instituted. Many people smoked in public and private gatherings. The Town Board informed the department smoking would no longer be allowed in the building.

At that same meeting, it was announced the *Women's Auxiliary Unit of the Patterson Fire Department No 1., Inc.* was formed. The Women's Auxiliary provided aid to the department. They also raised a significant amount of funds for the department. Funds raised by the Women's Auxiliary later helped purchase a new ambulance.

As military conflict intensified worldwide, calls for patriotism sounded out. At the November 3, 1941 meeting of the department, they accepted the invitation from the Putnam County Defense Council to march in a parade on November 11, which was called Armistice Day. That day was later renamed Veteran's Day.

The unexpected Imperial Japanese Empire's attack on Pearl Harbor took place on December 7, 1941. As a result of that attack 2,335 people died. The day after the horrific attack, President Franklin D. Roosevelt called it, *a day that would live in infamy.* He called for a declaration of war. Within an hour the United States Congress passed that declaration. Three days later, on December 11, 1941, Japan and Germany, who were already fighting England, Russia, and many other countries, declared war on the United States.

On January 6, 1942, the next meeting of the Patterson Fire Department after the attack on Pearl Harbor, the department voted to purchase $500 in Defense Bonds. Defense Bonds helped raise funds to produce military equipment. Throughout the war the department bought additional Defense Bonds. The department also approved a donation of $50 to the *American Red Cross* and $50 to the *Salvation Army* for their war relief efforts.

The department helped with local defense preparations during the war. On April 6, 1942, the department received a thank you letter from Dr. Albert Towner, expressing thanks for their *splendid cooperation* during the local air raid test. At that same meeting they voted not to hold a carnival due to the war. Carnivals did not resume until after the war in 1947.

The department was proud of its members who served during the war. At the May 4, 1942 meeting, they assigned a chart be made and posted in the hall of all members serving in the Army, Navy, and Marines.

As part of security concerns during the war, the department ordered all members to be fingerprinted on September 1, 1942.

At the October 4, 1942 meeting of the department a report was read from the New York State war Council regarding regulations during air raids and blackouts.

At the December 6, 1943 meeting, the department voted to encourage their servicemen by sending $5 to all members serving in the armed forces. That is the equivalent of $81.25 in 2021. They passed the same resolution again on November 6, 1944. Those gifts were appreciated by the soldiers.

At the February 5, 1945 meeting, a letter was read from John Schenck (spelling later changed to Schenk). It stating he was serving in the Army in Belgium and that he was in good health. He thanked the department for their kind remembrance at Christmas.

During that time Putnam Lake continued to grow, so did fire calls and the need for additional fire protection and firefighting equipment near that community. At the May 7, 1945 meeting of the Patterson Fire Department, they authorized the 1927 Hahn pumper be sent to join the 1921 Chemical Truck at Putnam Lake.

The department has always sought to acquire new equipment to help do a better job fighting fires. At the July 2, 1945 meeting, a new piece of equipment called a fog nozzle was demonstrated. A fog nozzle breaks the stream of water from a fire hose into smaller droplets. That covers greater surface area and smothers the fire by displacing its oxygen.

The next year after the department sent the Hahn pumper to Putnam Lake, at the November 5, 1946 meeting, $1,790 was approved to buy a new Dodge pumper to replace the Dodge Squad Wagon. At the May 6, 1946 meeting, that amount was increased to $1,900. That pumper was purchased. Years later that truck would be donated to the Putnam Lake Fire Department.

To help address the increased need for closer fire protection in Putnam Lake, on January 9, 1946, the Patterson Fire Department held a meeting at Putnam Lake. Chief Ferris J. Sprague presided. The department established a separate company there, with Frank

Huber appointed Foreman. Former Chief Junia Dykeman, Jr., instructed the new company in First Aid, Artificial Respiration, team work and other matters.

Six months later, at the July 1, 1946 meeting of the Patterson Fire Department, a resolution was made and approved to have Putnam Lake form their own fire department. On August 9, 1946, the Patterson Town Bord approved the formation of the Putnam Lake Department.

Dr. Joseph L. Peloso donated a small plot of land on Haviland Drive for the new Putnam Lake Fire Department to build a firehouse. The Warner Brothers donated three additional lots. Construction was started on the building and it was dedicated on May 30, 1948.

Kenneth A. Hall, who was originally a member of the Patterson Fire Department, lived in the new Putnam Lake firehouse as the resident fireman. He was a veteran of the Spanish American War. When a fire call came, he was ready and notified others to respond.

The Patterson Fire Department officially donated the 1921 Buffalo Chemical Truck to the newly formed Putnam Lake Fire Department. That truck saw active service in Putnam Lake for a number of years.

At the December 18, 1946 meeting of the Patterson Fire Department, there was a dispute over the naming of the Putnam Lake Fire Department. Some wanted it to be called *Patterson Fire Department, No. 2*. After a discussion, they agreed to accept the town's designation of the new department as the *Putnam Lake Fire Department*. They also agreed to approve the transfer of all members who wanted to join that department.

At the January 4, 1948 meeting of the department, they approved buying another new piece of equipment, their first portable pump. Portable pumps are helpful pumping out flooded buildings and are frequently used by the department to the present day.

At the February 2, 1948 meeting of the department, fourteen years after the department authorized a committee to look at building a firehouse, Charles Van Keuren introduced a resolution to start a building fund to build a firehouse for the department. The resolution passed. Yet, it would take another 20 years before that firehouse would be built. When the firehouse was built, that same Charles Van Keuren was the department's President.

Throughout the years there were many resolutions regarding uniforms. At the February 23, 1948 meeting, it was determined the cost of uniforms rose from $38.25 to $41.75. They approved having the members pay $5 down and then $5 per month until their uniform was paid in full. At the April 5, 1948 meeting, that was changed to require a $20 deposit.

One of the challenges firefighters encounter when responding to calls is trying to get to the firehouse quickly and safely. A big obstacle to that is other drivers on the road. Volunteer firefighters are not allowed to have sirens on their cars. Decals or brass plaques identifying them as members of the fire department do not do much to alert other drivers. In 1949, to help firefighters have a way to alert other drivers they are responding to a call, New York

State authorized firemen to use blue lights when responding to calls. A representative of the *Firemen's Blue Light Company* from Pawling, New York came to the department's monthly meeting on May 2, 1949 and demonstrated some lights.

For many years the Patterson Fire Department provided ambulance service to residents of the town. At the August 15, 1949 meeting, it was reported an ambulance was donated to the department, free and clear, however it needed extensive repairs. They agreed to determine a price for those repairs. At the September 5, 1949 meeting, it was reported the repairs would cost $567.81. The department voted to sell the ambulance and give the funds to the Women's Auxiliary to buy another ambulance. They were not able to sell that ambulance. They finally junked it and received $25.

On November 7, 1949, as the Cold War intensified, it was decided all members of the department would have their blood tested by the Red Cross and placed on file for emergency purposes.

The next year, on September 4, 1950, the Women's Auxiliary asked for a loan to purchase another ambulance. On October 18, 1950, a special meeting was held to discuss ambulances with representatives from Buick and Cadillac. The department favored the Cadillac, which was priced at $7,218.35, before extra equipment was added. After adding equipment, minus a resuscitator, which the department already owned (pictured here), the price came to $7,392.60. The order was placed on October 25, 1950.

The garage, which the town allowed the department to use to house its vehicles, was too small to house two fire engines and an ambulance. On January 1, 1951 the department approved a motion to ask the town to add an addition of 24' to the firehouse. It does not appear that addition was ever built. Instead they used the garage of the liquor distributor. Later, the ambulance was parked in the garage at member Willie Boone's house. Willie later became Chief of the Department.

As part of the recreational aspect of belonging to the fire department, on November 5, 1951 the department approved buying baseball bats from Lynch's Store for the department. In September, it was reported the cost for the baseball bats was $11.20.

When the department started in 1921, firemen were summoned to calls by a work whistle mounted on top of the Pendleton and Townsend Factory, where the fire departments apparatus was housed. Twenty-eight years later, on April 30, 1956, the department authorized a more technologically advanced method of summoning its' members. It approved installing telephones in the homes of all its members so they could be notified of fire calls. At the May 6, 1957 meeting, it was reported the phones were installed and should be operational soon. The phone system was operational by August 1957. Members were instructed the phones were only to be used for fire department business.

In 1971, another new form of technology was adopted. A short wave radio base station was added to the firehouse. That greatly increased the efficiency of notifying firefighters and provided communication between apparatus. Today a modern radio alert system is used, combined with an internet application, which can summon fire, medical, and auxiliary personnel, within seconds of a call for help.

Keeping with technological advances, in January 1956, the department added an enjoyable benefit to its members, it bought its first television.

One important aspect of fire departments is providing scene safety. In 1939, New York State passed a law allowing fire departments to officially designate people as fire police. Fire Police assist with scene safety and are designated as Peace Officers, with law enforcement and arrest powers by the state.

At the June 6, 1956, meeting of the Patterson Fire Department it was announced the New York State Police started to provide official training for Fire Police. The Patterson Fire Department sent men to receive that training and have continued to do so for many years. A number of women n the department took that training and serve on the Fire Police Team.

At that same meeting, in June 1956 the department looked at specifications for a new piece of fire apparatus. Two months later, as the August 6, 1956 meeting, they modified the specifications for a new fire truck. Three months later, on November 12, 1956, the department authorized $17,439 to buy a new Mack.

At a special meeting on July 5, 1957, it was announced they still did not have enough funds

to buy the new Mack. It was proposed and approved the department would borrow the money from the Building Fund and pay it back at 4%. At the August 5, 1957 meeting Milt Kessman offered to loan the department the funds they needed for the truck at 3% interest, if the department gave him the old 1927 Hahn. At the November 4, 1957 meeting the department approved borrowing the money from Kessman at 3% interest for 4 years, and approved giving him the Hahn. At the March 3, 1958 meeting the price of the new Mack was presented as $17,682. They borrowed $5,000 from Milt Kessman and $1,000 from the Building funds. The rest they had in a truck fund from fund raising.

From the beginning, the Patterson Fire Department used many fund raising methods. One of the more unique fund raising methods the department used started in the 1920's. The department formed *The Patterson Fire Department Minstrels*. The Minstrels were formed in the early 1920's and performed various musical shows throughout the 1920's-1940's to help raise funds. In later years the department conducted numerous dances, parties, comedy shows, and book sales. It even did Donkey Basketball and Donkey Softball.

At the April 7, 1958 meeting, the department discussed the idea of having Associate Members. Those members would help around the firehouse and with activities but would not respond to calls. Two months later, at the June 2, 1959 meeting, the role of Associate Members were officially created.

For many years the Patterson Fire Department sought to have its own firehouse. It formed committees and raised funds. The garage used to store the trucks was small and trucks had

to be stored in the garage of the liquor distributor next door. No real progress was made on getting a new building until 1968, when Stahl Hall, home for the department since 1921 was condemned. The department had no choice, it had to move. Land was acquired from Fred Dill across the railroad tracks, on the south side of on Main Street (later called Route 311). Construction began immediately and the department moved into the building in 1968 before it was completed because Stahl Hall was demolished.

That new building became a much appreciated firehouse with four apparatus bays, offices, and a meeting room. For more than twenty years it served as home to the department as the town and its needs for greater fire protection rapidly grew.

After moving into the new firehouse in 1968, the department bought a few used vehicles to help with its fire-fighting. A used 1950's International R Series Tanker was purchased. It was an oil truck which was converted and used as a water tanker to provide more water on scene to help fight fires. The department bought another used oil truck. It was a 1967 International Tanker.

1951 International Tanker Repainted Red

When Robert Smith, Sr. was chief, the department bought a used 1951 Mack Open Cab Fire Engine from the Hicksville, New York Fire Department. It served the department well for a number of years. That was the last used firefighting apparatus the department purchased.

One factor the department had to consider back then, and even today, with the purchase of any new vehicles, was their height. The new firehouse had tall enough bays to accommodate most fire-fighting apparatus available at that time but there are bridges with low clearance in town. One is on Route 311. The other two are on Route 164. They have old railroad bridges with low clearance which makes it impossible for taller vehicles, including some fire-fighting apparatus, to pass under. Those bridges required the fire department back then, and today, to get vehicles with low enough clearance so they can pass under those bridges as they respond to calls. Many neighboring departments have apparatus which are too tall to make it under those bridges.

Though the new firehouse was sufficient for its day, three factors had a significant impact on the department and would cause their new firehouse to become obsolete. The first had to do with the construction of Interstates 84 and 684. Before 1963, there were three ways to cross the Hudson River from this area. One was to go north and west on N.Y. Route 55 to Poughkeepsie and then cross the Mid-Hudson Bridge. Another was to go south and west on Route 6 and cross the Bear Mountain Bridge. The third was to go west on N.Y. Route 52 from Carmel and cross the Hudson River at Beacon by Ferry. The volume of cars and trucks going east and west, through Patterson was minimal.

The main east-west route going from Massachusetts to California in the 1960's was U.S. Route 6. For many years it was known as the *Wagon Train Road* because it carried Conestoga Covered Wagons from Massachusetts to the Midwest. After the War Between the States it was given the name, *The Grand Army of the Republic Highway*, to honor veterans from the war. It then extended all the way to California. That road does not go through Patterson, but traffic patterns were about to change.

In 1963, New York State started construction of a major east-west highway through the Hudson Valley in order to help alleviate traffic through New York City and lower Westchester County. That year, they built the *Newburgh-Beacon Bridge* across the Hudson River and started construction of Interstate 84.

Postcard of the New Newburgh-Beacon Bridge, c. 1962

In 1963, N.Y. Route 9, the Taconic Parkway, and N.Y. Route 22 were the three north-south New York State roads. In 1964, the state started to construct Interstate 87 as its main north-south route. Construction did not start where I-87 is today. It started north along Route 22 from New York City. In 1969, the year after the Patterson Fire Department built its firehouse, I-87 opened as a four lane highway from New York City to Brewster. That made it much easier and much faster to get from Patterson to Westchester County and New York City. On January 1, 1970, the New York State Thruway, heading north out of New York City was designated as I-87 and the old I-87 which terminated in Brewster was renamed I-684.

In 1970, two years after the Patterson Fire Department moved into its new firehouse, I-84, which crossed the Hudson River in 1963, reached N.Y. Route 311 in Patterson. In 1971, I-84 was connected to I-684 in Brewster and completed to the Connecticut state line. The connecting, and opening, of those two interstates immediately brought thousands of cars and trucks through Patterson every day.

The drastic increase in traffic, cause by the interstates, brought an increase in accidents on both sections of those roads in Patterson. Many of those accidents included vehicles traveling at a much faster rate of speed than on the old roads. Large commercial vehicles, using those roads, increased the severity of the accidents.

The Patterson Fire Department is responsible for providing emergency services on NY 22 and on the portion of I-84 which goes through the town. For many years, the Patterson Fire Department struggled to handle the increased demand, along with the more serious nature of those accidents. By 1988, the department bought a large new 1988 Mack Rescue Truck to provide better service. That created another challenge. The firehouse could no longer house all the department's vehicles.

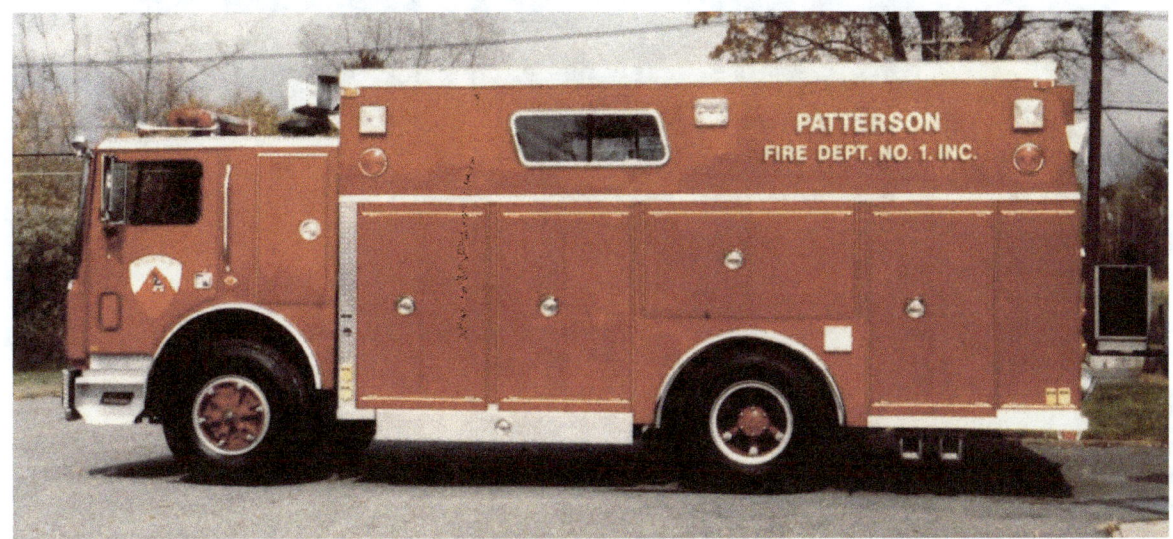

1988 Mack Rescue Truck

The second factor, which effected the fire department back then, was the fact that I-84 and I-684 made the commute to Patterson from New York City and lower Westchester much faster. That resulted in a huge influx of people moving to Patterson and the surrounding area. That caused a rapid increase in the population, and a greater demand for fire and emergency services.

A third factor which effected the Fire Department, was the purchase of the Mendel Farm by the *Watchtower Bible and Tract Society*, better known as the *Jehovah's Witnesses*. That group purchased that property to build a campus with 27 buildings. One of the buildings they wanted to build was tall and required the local fire department have a ladder truck. That was something the Patterson Fire Department did not have.

In 1988, to secure approval for their project, the Jehovah's Witnesses helped buy a 100 foot ladder truck for the Patterson Fire Department. That created a challenge for the department. The new truck was too long to fit in any of the bays at the firehouse. That prompted the department to build a new firehouse on the land it already owned on Burdick Road, across Route 311 from the firehouse built in 1968.

The new firehouse was built in 1991 when Charlie Smyth was President of the department. It has eight bays on Burdick Road, including an extra-long bay to house the ladder truck. It also had two bays on a lower level, facing Route 311, which housed the department's ambulance.

Groundbreaking for Current Firehouse

The Jehovah's Witnesses also helped the department build a picnic pavilion on the new property. That pavilion is a great addition which has been used for many activities for the department and the community. It is the site of the annual Relay for Life which helps raise funds to fight cancer. It has also been used for the Fire Department's Giant Book Sale.

Many people do not realize the new firehouse, which is the current home to the Patterson Fire Department, is located adjacent to the old Sheffield Ice Pond, the first property the purchased back in 1933.

Over the years, as the department marched in different parades, it hired marching bands to march with them. In 1971, the department formed its own junior marching band called *The Yellow Jackets*. Many young people joined. They marched with the department in numerous parades until they disbanded a few years later. The band equipment was sold to the Lake Carmel and Putnam Lake Fire Departments.

The department has always sought to add new, more effective equipment to it arsenal of fire-fighting tools. In 1979, they added a Lucas Hydraulic Spreader Tool. It is often referred to as *the jaws of life*. That tool is used to cut through a car when someone is trapped.

In 1999, the department added another new state of the art, piece of equipment called a thermal imaging camera. That camera detects heat signatures. It allows firefighters to see possible fires behind walls. It can also help locate people.

Patterson Fire Department has always been a welcoming department to people, no matter their ethnic, racial, or religious background. From the very first year, the department has always had immigrants among its members, as well as people of different religious groups.

That welcoming has not always been the case in Putnam County. In some towns racism and discrimination were strong. Immigrants, Catholics, Jews, and people of color were treated poorly throughout the county. The Ku Klux Klan (KKK), a white supremacist group started after the Civil War by the Democrats in the south, found a strong following in Putnam County. Some of the largest Klan rallies in America were held in Philipstown and Cold Spring, on the west side of Putnam County. The Grange in Patterson even debated if they should allow *Blacks* to belong.

While racism was rampant in the 1960's and 1970's, and African-Americans were not welcome in some places, they were welcome in the Patterson Fire Department. The department had a number of African American members. In the 1960 film, "*Our Town,*" twelve members of the Patterson Fire Department appear, including Harry Freeman, an African-American member of the department.

In 1970, when Patterson Fire Department choose its chief, it choose Willie C. Boone, Jr. (pictured here), who is African American. He was chosen, not because of his race but because he was considered the most qualified man to lead the department. He was also said to be one of the most respected men in town. Chief Boone is still regarded by many as one of the best chiefs the department ever had.

In a county where prejudice was intense against Jews, in 1974, the Patterson Fire Department disregarded that. They not only welcomed S. Delvalle Goldsmith, who was Jewish, but even though most people in the department were Catholic or Protestant, they elected him to serve as Chaplain of the department. He was also elected Vice-President. He was so respected, the current firehouse was named after him.

The Patterson Fire Department has always been impacted by social issues but also by world events. On September 11, 2001, Islamic terrorists hijacked four commercial airplanes and launched the worst attack on American soil since Pearl Harbor. They flew two airplanes into the Twin Towers of the World Trade Center in New York City and one into the Pentagon in Washington, D.C. The passengers in the fourth airplane the terrorists hijacked, overpowered the terrorists as it flew over Shanksville, Pennsylvania, before they could strike their third target. They heroically gave their lives to save others.

Just as members of the Patterson Fire Department bravely respond to fire calls, as the Twin Towers burned, brave New York City Firefighters and Police officers hurried to the site and entered the buildings and began rescue operations. Hundreds of thousands of lives were saved thanks to their heroic efforts. Two hours and forty-two minutes after the first plane hit the towers, both towers, along with nearby buildings in the World Trade Center, collapsed. A total of 2,763 people lost their lives, including 343 first responders.

Arrival of the Large Piece of Steel from 9-11 for our Memorial

Firefighters from the surrounding area hurried to the scene to assist in rescue efforts. Fire Departments in the surrounding areas, including Patterson, were activated to provide coverage. Chief Adam Stiebeling brought the department's ladder truck to the scene along with other members of the department. In appreciation of their role, the Patterson Fire Department received a piece of steel from the site of the attack. That piece was placed next to the firehouse as a memorial to those who gave their lives on 9-11.

The Patterson Fire Department has always strived to not only protect the people of Patterson but to help others in need. In August 2005, Hurricane Katrina, a category five storm, hit the south and devastated the Gulf Coast. It killed more than 1,800 people and caused more than $125 billion in damage. New Orleans and the surrounding areas in Louisiana and Mississippi were hardest hit.

In response to that disaster, the Patterson Fire Department lead a drive to gather supplies to help the people in the Town of Waveland, Mississippi. Waveland is 58 miles east of New Orleans. On Sunday October 23, 2005, the department loaded its

1977 Oren Fire Engine with firefighting supplies, as well as supplies for schools and churches. Chaplain Paul Maass then lead the department in a prayer for the people of Waveland. Some members of the department went with the fire engine and made the presentation of the engine and its supplies to the people of Waveland. Chief Bob Smith, Sr., went south to Waveland and delivered the Oren and supplies.

John Simpson, one of the members of the department, went south with the Department of Homeland Security to help with the recovery efforts. While there he adopted a dog who was orphaned by the hurricane and named her *Katrina* (pictured). When he returned north, *Katrina* often visited the firehouse, along with *Beekman*, another rescue dog John adopted.

Since the Patterson Fire Department was formed in 1921, the population of the town has increased almost ten-fold. The need for emergency response and fire protection increased significantly. The fire department grew from one department with two vehicles to two different fire departments, one on each side of town. The two departments have more than 15 vehicles they use to help fight fires.

Many people are not aware the Patterson Fire Department, along with the Putnam Lake Fire Department, have always been volunteer organizations. Their volunteering has saved taxpayers millions of dollars, which is what it would have cost if the town had a paid fire department. Another fact which may surprise many people is the budget for the Patterson Library is larger than the budget for the Patterson Fire Department.

Over the years, members of the community joined both departments and gave hundreds of hours courageously providing rescue and fire protection to our community. At one time the department had more than 100 members and two ambulances. As the years passed, the factories and many businesses in town closed. Though more people moved to the town, many commuted out of town for work. Those factors, combined with rising taxes and the skyrocketing cost of living, made it so many people had to work more than one job to make ends meet. That makes volunteering more difficult. The number of people volunteering has drastically declined. That reduction in volunteers affects the fire department.

The reduction in volunteers made it especially difficult to provide a full crew to staff an ambulance during the day. It came to the point where the town had to contract with a paid ambulance company to provide ambulance service during the day. That resulted in people being charged when they called an ambulance. The fire department provided service during the evening and weekends. The town eventually formed its own paid ambulance service. The fire department ambulance became available on a second call basis during the day and provided a crew during some evenings. As a result of that change the department eliminated its second ambulance. The need for new volunteers to maintain effective fire and rescue services to the people in town is greater than ever.

The Patterson Fire Department No. 1 now has two firehouses. The main one is located on Burdick Road, just off Route 311. It has eight bays for fire apparatus along with two ambulance bays. The department also has a sub-station on Bullet Hole Road with two large doors, with a total of four bays. The Putnam Lake Fire Department has seven bays.

Fire vehicles at the Patterson Fire Department increased over the years from that first old chemical truck to multiple complex and technologically advanced vehicles, equipped with the latest firefighting features. Those vehicles include a 100' fire ladder truck, engines, tanker, heavy rescue, brush truck, ambulance, all-terrain vehicle, a fire police truck and three chief's vehicles.

In 2020, the Corona Virus, which originated in Wuhan, in Communist China, quickly spread around the world causing a pandemic. President Donald Trump shut down travel from China and then travel from other countries around the world where the virus was spreading and killing hundreds of thousands of people. In March 2020, the President also implemented shutdowns in the United States and asked everyone to wear face masks and maintain social distancing. That shutdown closed schools, businesses, and public gatherings all across the country. Fear gripped many people as thousands died. Newly elected President Joe Biden continued the shutdown. Hundreds of thousands, especially the elderly, continued to die. Three vaccines, to protect people from the virus were quickly developed with the support of President Trump and received unprecedented approval. Administration of the vaccine's began under President Trump and continued under President Biden. As a greater percentage of the population were vaccinated, the number of reported infections and death decreased and the shutdown began to be lifted.

During the pandemic, the Patterson Fire Department was required to suspend all in-person gatherings and drills because of concerns over the possibility of spreading the virus. Regardless of the shutdown, and perhaps in some cases precipitated by it, calls for accidents, fires, and emergencies still came in. The members of our department responded bravely and faithfully to all the calls wearing face masks, personal protective equipment, and maintaining social distancing. The pandemic delayed monthly meetings and elections. Some meetings were held at the Patterson Recreation Center because the meeting room n the firehouse did not meet state guidelines to provide proper social distancing. It was not until May 3, 2021, as the effects of the pandemic began to subside, that the department was able to hold an in-person monthly meeting back at the firehouse.

For 100 years the Patterson Department has served its community through wars, peace time and through a national pandemic. We would love to have more people join us, and our friends at the Putnam Lake Fire Department as we continue to serve for many more years.

Our Buildings
Our First Home

Stahl's Hall

Department Garage

The first home of the Patterson Fire Department was Stahl's Hall on Main Street. It was formed there in 1921 and remained in that building until 1968. In 1921, the first floor of Stahl's Hall was used as the Town Hall. The fire apparatus was kept at the boiler annex of the *Pendleton & Townsend Sash Company* from 1921 until 1927. In 1927, the town allowed the fire department to use a small garage located next to Stahl's Hall, for its apparatus. The above picture, on the left, shows Stahl's Hall in 1968. The fire bell can be seen on top of the building, where there used to be a steeple. The picture on the right shows our 1962 Cadillac ambulance, in front of our first garage and second home for our apparatus.

Members on our 1937 Mack in Front of the First Garage on Main Street
Junia Dykeman, William Bubinicek, Frank Lyden Sr., and Henry Ludington in White Hats

Our Second Home and Our Own Firehouse

Our second home was the first firehouse we owned. It was built in 1968 across the railroad tracks on the south side of Main Street (Route 311). After the department moved from there to its third home, across the road, this building was renovated and became home to the Patterson Justice Court and the Patterson Library. The Justice Court later moved to its own building. The building was renovated and is now exclusively the home of the Patterson Library.

Our Current Firehouse

Our current firehouse, known as Station One, was built in 1991 on Burdick Road, alongside Route 311 (Main Street). The building is basically two stories but comprised of three levels. The lowest level features two ambulance bays, an ambulance squad room, a large storage area for equipment, and a fitness area. The second level, facing Burdick Road, features eight bays, a radio room, offices, and firefighter equipment racks. The third level consists of a Recreation Room, Kitchen, Large Meeting Room, office, and a smaller meeting room. In 2006, Station 1 was dedicated in honor of S. Delvalle "Del" Goldsmith.

Exercise Room

Recreation Room
Bob Johnson, John Radtke, Patrick O'Connell, Bob Bell

Picnic Pavilion

9-11 Memorial

Our department was part of the joint emergency response to the September 11, 2001 terrorist attacks on the World Trade Center in New York City. Our memorial includes a piece of steel from the World Trade Center.

Sub-Station 2

Sub-Station 2 was built in 1976. It is located on Bullet Hole Road, near the Fox Run Housing Complex. That was the largest development in Patterson at the time. This Sub-Station has two large doors with two bays each. It can house four vehicles.

Our Fire Fighting Vehicles Over the Years

In May of 1921, our department's first new vehicle was a modern Buffalo Chemical Fire Apparatus mounted on an Oldsmobile chassis. Over the years we added numerous vehicles which provided many years of faithful service. Our first vehicles were red. Later we changed to lime green trucks, which look yellow. We then changed back to red.

Our First New Vehicle a 1921 Buffalo Chemical Truck
Members on the Truck

1930's Photo of our 1927 Hahn and 1932 Dodge Fire Trucks

Our 1932 Dodge "Squad Wagon" in a Parade

Our 1937 Mack and 1932 Dodge in Front of Our Old Garage

Our 1946 Dodge Pumper
This Photo Was Taken After it Was Given to the Putnam Lake Fire Department

1937 Mack Type 25E – Patterson Engine 80
Bought New – Converted to a Brush Truck in 1969

Original 1958 Mack
Purchased New

Original 1958 Mack – Patterson Engine 78
With New Pump Controls & New Logo Added

1950's International R-Series Tanker- Yellow then Painted Red
A Used Oil Truck Converted to Water Tanker

1951 Mack Open Cab – Patterson Engine 79
Acquired Used in the 1970's from Hicksville, Long Island

1967 International Tanker– Patterson Tanker 76
A Used Oil Truck Converted to a Water Tanker

1971 Interntional Fleetstar Engine
Bought New

1971 International Fleetstar Engine
Same Truck as Above with New Logo & Raised Wall with 5" Hose Added

1968 International Loadstar Tanker

1976 FMC Engine

1970's Dodge Powerwagon Brush Truck

1986 International S Series Tanker

1977 Oren Engine – Yellow

1977 Oren Engine – Same as Above Repainted Red

2000 Sutphen Engine 22-2-3

1998 Sutphen Big Red Machine 22-4-2

1989 Sutphen 100' Ladder Truck

2013 ATV Ranger 800EFI Emergency Response Vehicle

1994 Sutphen Engine 22-2-1

1996 Sutphen Engine 22-5-1

Our Second Rescue Truck – A Used 1957 Ford

Our Third Rescue Truck – A New 1988 Mack

Our Fourth Rescue Truck - 2010 Spartan

Ford F250 Brush Truck

1986 Jeep Brush Truck

1988 GMC Fire Police Truck 22-8-1

1984 Ford Esort
Personal Chief's Vehicle

1989 Chevy K5 Blazer
1st Dept, Owned Chief's Vehicle

1997 GMC Chief's Vehicle

2013 Chevy Tahoe Chief's Vehicle

2015 Chief's Vehicle

2021 Chevrolet Chief's Vehicle

Our Equipment & Turn Out Gear

The equipment and turn out gear, used by this department, has changed significantly. Its main role is to protect the firefighter so they can do their job.
The Chief's Hat pictured below helped save Chief Adam Steibeling in a fire.

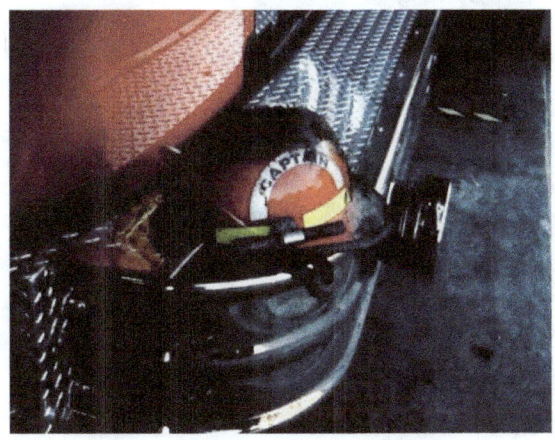
Adam Steibleing's Helmet

Old Helmet Badge

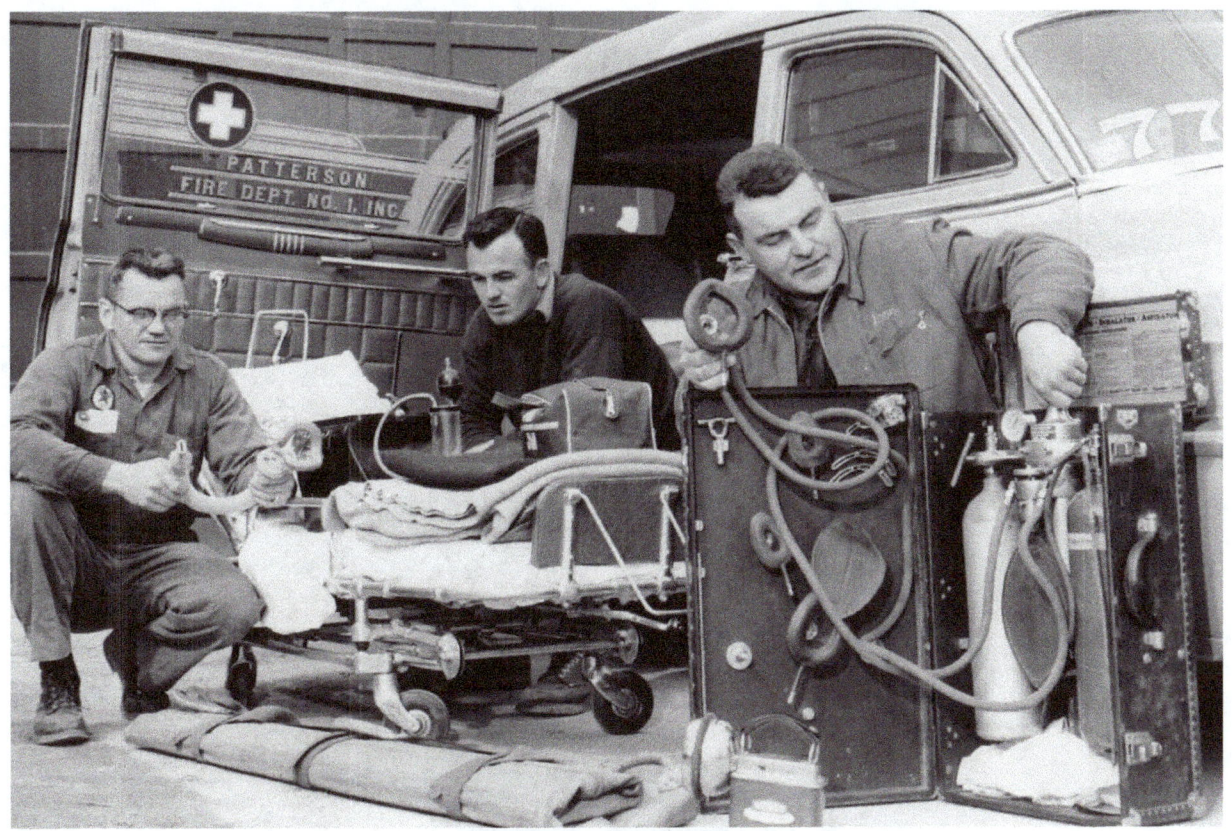
Bill Millar, Roy Covell, and Donald Smith with Ambulance Gear

George Apap and Willie Boone at Engine Pump Controls

Del Goldsmith's Helmet

Firefighters wearing their Turnout Gear
Raul Vielman, Rick Bosser, Kyle Fredericks, Zachary Mulkins,
Matthew Szpindor, Joe Pignatelli, Brian Vonditsh, Andrew Aiken

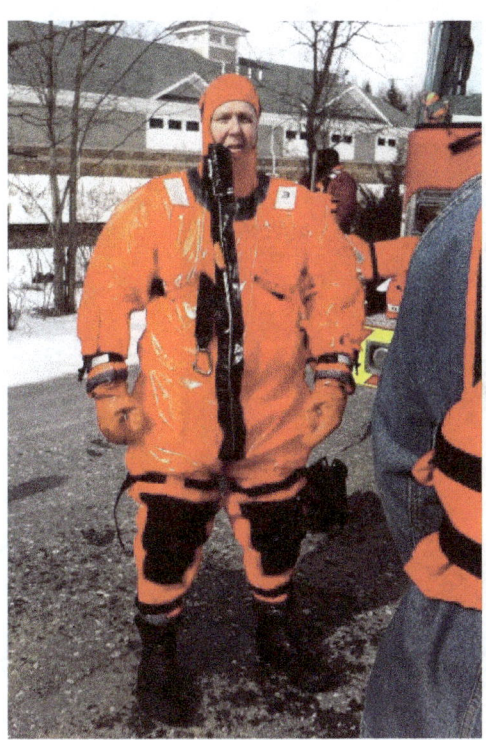

John Simpson in Ice Rescue Suit

Raft for Ice Rescue

Power Rescue Tools

Air Bottles Used by Firefighters

John Simpson with Face Mask

Cutting Car with Power Rescue Tool

Inspecting Tools from the Rescue Truck
Chris Van Name, Vinny Montouro, Matt Szpindor

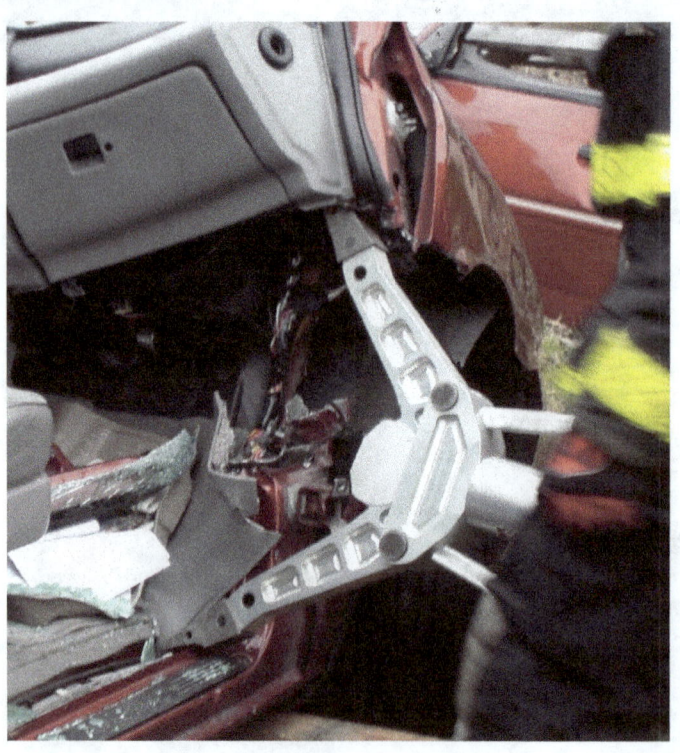

EMT Cody Hickok with Turn Out Bag

Our Fire Police

Fire Police have existed in New York State as early as 1839. Fire Police help with traffic control and scene safety. In 1939, New York State passed a law authorizing Fire Departments to form their own Fire Police. Many departments assigned the task to older members who could no longer fight fires. There were Fire Police in the Patterson Fire Department since 1939. In 1974, John Bodor formed a new Fire Police Squad with both younger and older members who received specialized training and Fire Police uniforms. In 1979, New York State made the requirements and training for Fire Police more stringent. Fire Police were designated as Peace Officers. Each one is registered annually with the *New York State Registry of Police and Peace Officers* and are now New York State Fire Police.

The Fire Police Squad in 1974
George Apap, Mike Semo, Del Goldsmith, John Bodor, George Gronke, Ed Centofante

John Bodor

Paul Maass, Phil Porcelli

Nelson Barrett, George Apap, Del Goldsmith, Charlie Smyth, Phil Porcelli, Ed Centofante, John Bodor, Mike Semo

Del Goldsmith, Marie Gronke, Ed Centofante, Pat Apap, Pat Semo, Mary Bodor
John Bodor, Mike Semo, George Apap

Frank Brunow Sr., Roger Tricinelli, Phil Porcelli & Ed Farrell

Our Rescue & Ambulance Squad

The Patterson Fire Department provided rescue services since its inception, In February 1951, the department purchased a new Cadillac ambulance, with funds raised by the Women's Auxiliary. Since then it had a number of different new ambulances. It is not unusual for the Ambulance Squad to receive more than one hundred calls a year. Each call requires a minimum of a driver and a certified Emergency Medical Technician (EMT).

Our New 1951 Cadillac Ambulance

Our 1962 Cadillac Ambulance

Our 1971 International Ambulance

After the next ambulance was purchased this became **Our First Rescue Vehicle**

Ford Econoline Ambulance

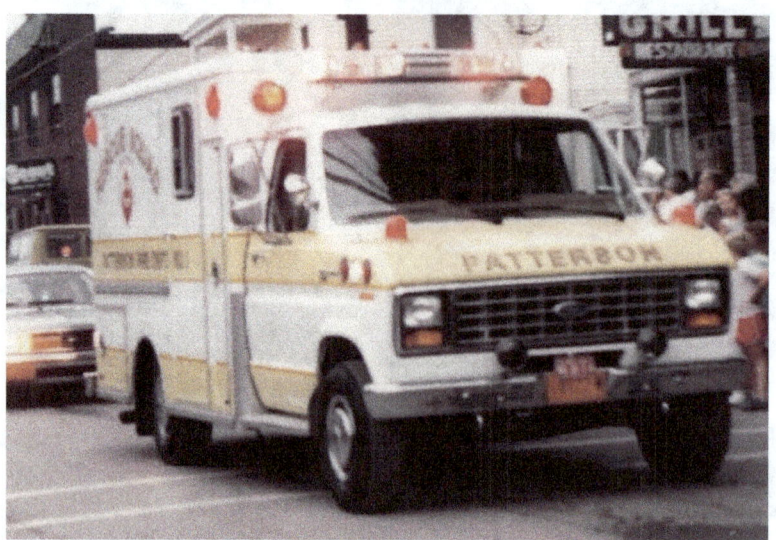

Ford Modular Ambulance

Ford Modular Ambulance

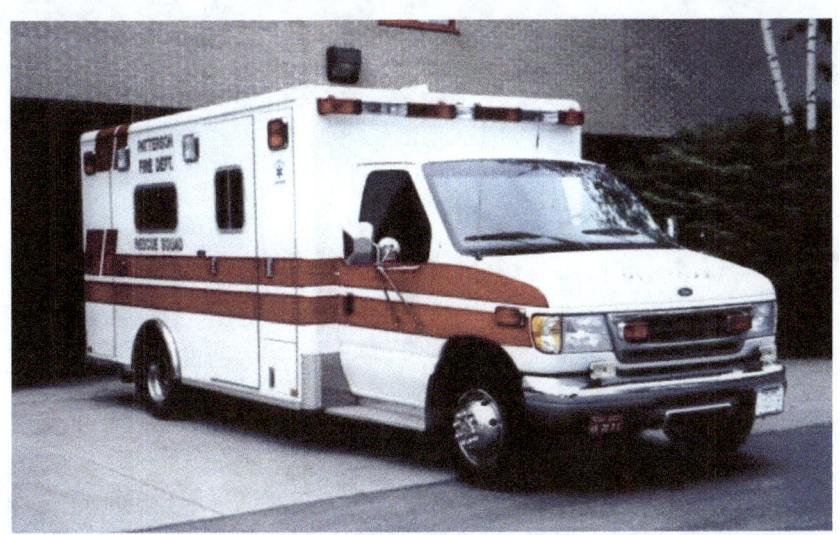

1998 Ford Ambulance

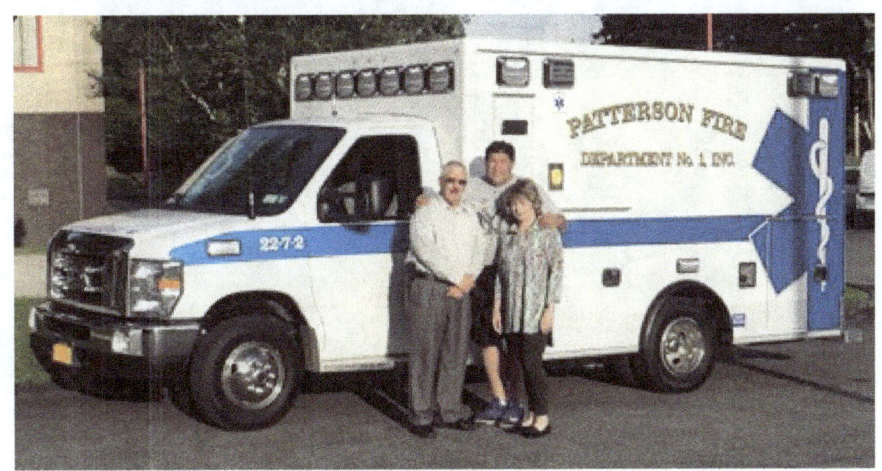

2016 Ford Ambulance
Bob Cuomo, Mario Gabrielli, Diane Vishinski

Tim Smith, Brian Burdick, Diane Vishinski, Cindy Covell, Bob Smith Jr., Tracy Smith, Bert Gonci, Rick Bosser, Cathy Davis, Sheri Citrone, Bob Cuomo, Tommy Lee, Jimmy Piazza

Patterson Fire Department Women's Auxiliary

The Patterson Fire Department Women's Auxiliary No 1, Inc., is a separate organization. Members of the Women's Auxiliary provided much appreciated meals, coffee, and aid to firefighters during and after calls. They also helped raise funds and helped purchase equipment, like our first ambulance. They also run a scholarship fund.

Mary Smith, Dolly Williams, Ann Wadle, Anna Baker, Juile Boone

Tootsie Petersen, Jenny Renak, Marie Gronke, Ann Baker, Rose Perrin, Dorothy Hayden, Ann Wadle, Freeman, Alice Smith, Julia Boone, Judy Baker, Jessie Cole, Esther Covell

Julia Boone, Roe Perrin, Jessie Cole, Alice Smith, Trudy Mill

Carol Isherwood, Trudy Mill, Ann Wadle, Mary O'Connell, Bev Lauro, Bridget Pasko

Beverly Lauro, Donna Hazzard, Mary O'Connell

Pat Brown, Marie Gronke, Pat Semo, Mary Bodor

Ann Johnson, Beverly Lauro, Marlene Fischer, Jessie Cole, Donna Hazard, Judy Piazza

Mary O'Connell, Trudy Mill, Pat Semo, Donna Hazard, Beverly Lauro

Pat Brown, Mary Bodor, Marie Gronke, Pat Semo

Trudy Mill, Liz Krepel, Marie Gronke, Mary Bodor

Rose Perrin, Mary O'Connell, Bev Lauro

Lori Racki, Mary Brown, Eileen Casey, Tracy Holland

Rose Perrin, Trudy Mill, Mary Bodor, Mary Gronke

Mary O'Connell, Bev Lauro, Tammy, Tim Smith, Tonianne Bourke, Mary Brown, Lori Racki, Tracy Holland, Stephine Goetz, Cindy Covell, Heather Fredericks

Organizations Within the Department
The Minstrels - Yellow Jackets Marching Band
Ski Team – Bowling Team - Softball Team

Over the years the Patterson Fire Department formed various organizations. In the 1920-1940's we had a group called **The Minstrels.** They conducted plays and concerts to raise funds for the department.

The Patterson Fire Department Minstrels 1929
The Members of the Minstrels at a Show They Conducted in the Old Town Hall

In 1971 we formed our own junior marching fife and drum corps called **The Yellow Jackets**. They marched with our department in parades. Anna Baker taught them fife.

The Yellow Jackets Marching Band
Anna Baker, Shirley Agar, Mike Colt, Paul Kessman, Joan Costello, Suzanne Agar

Yellow Jackets on Parade

Yellow Jackets Emblem

Sports Teams

Our department has had various sports teams including a bowling team, men's ski team, women's ski team, baseball team, and a softball team.

The Patterson Fire Department Softball Team
Lee Conway, Matt Kelly, Tommy Lee, Russell Mulkins, Brian Christian,
Steve Colt, P.J. O'Connell, Mike Smyth, Robert Smith Jr.

Putnam Lake Fire Department

On August 9, 1946 the Putnam Lake Fire Department was officially formed by the Town of Patterson. Putnam Lake is part of the Town of Patterson. In 1948, they moved into their first building. In 1951, the second floor was added. The firehouse was later expanded to include seven bays. Their fire vehicles were first red. They then transitioned to lime green (yellow). The Patterson Fire Department and the Putnam Lake Fire Department work together throughout the Town of Patterson.

Putnam Lake's First Firehouse

Putnam Lake's Expanded Current Firehouse

Our Members Training

All personnel in the Patterson Fire Department, including Firefighters, Fire Police and Ambulance Squad Workers, receive extensive training before they can serve. That initial training is followed by ongoing training which includes drills and special classes.

Chief Robert Bell teaching vehicle extrication Drill

Robert Barto demonstrates Stirrup Pump for firefighting at Merrick Farm

Our Firefighters receiving training at the Putnam County Training Facility

Ice Rescue Suits
Wilson Cajas, Albert Rossi, Brett Politi, Gene Boo

Demonstrating Equipment
Raul Vielman, Ricky Montana, Brandy Telesco

Tom Dixon, Kurt Vondietsch, Chris Van Name, Ed O'Connell, Stavros, Caleb Smith, Chris Brown, David Nunez, John & Chris Deitz, Justin Shepps Vinny Montouro, Matt Szpindor, Sheri Citrone, Raul Vielman

Pete O'Mara, Jimmy Fredericks, Eleanora Smith, Brian Vigliotti, Chris Deitz

Training on an MTA Train

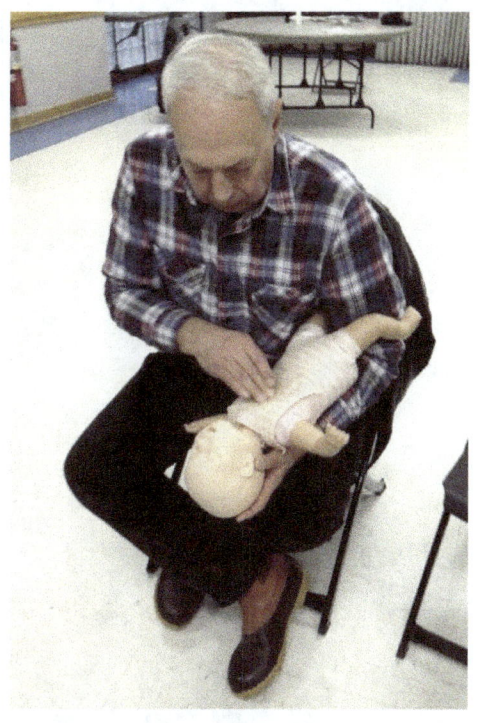

Phil Porcelli - Infant CPR Training

 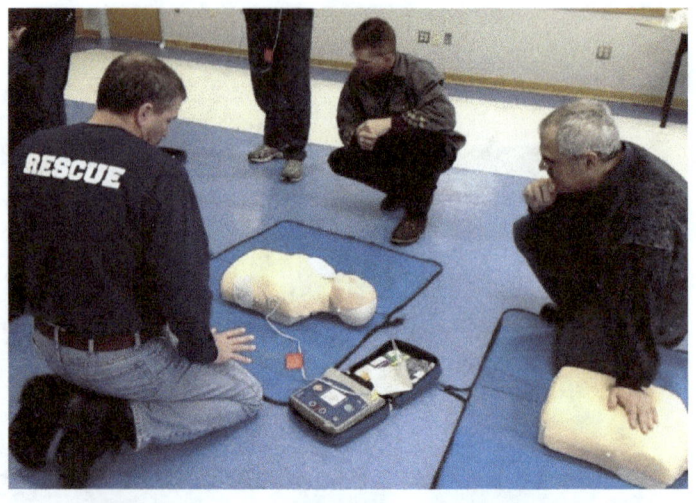

Jessica Smith Doing Bailout   CPR & AED Instructor, Tommy Gamache, Bob Cuomo

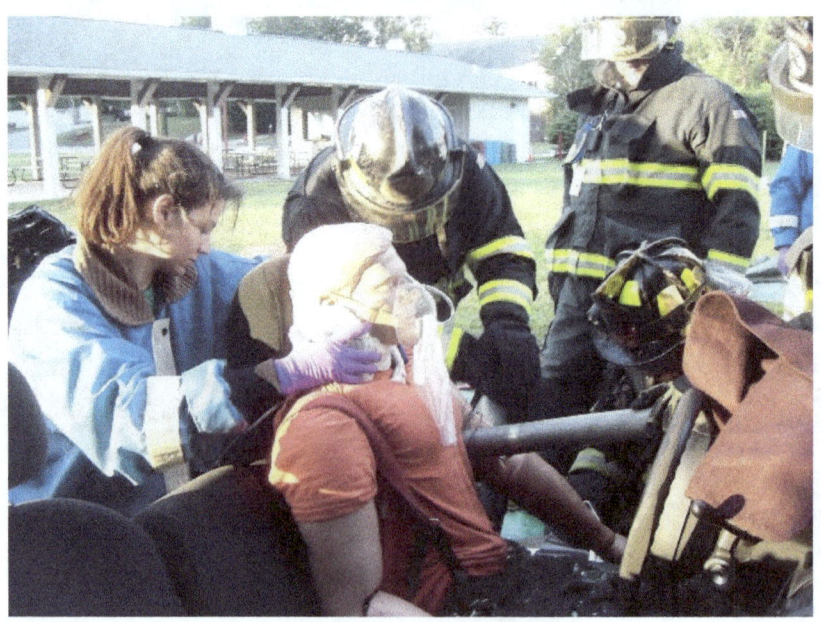

Extrication Drill

Water Rescue Training   Brandy Telesco, Joey Nickischer, Zach Mulkins

Joint Drill with Putnam Lake Fire Department On Vehicle Extrication

Assistant Chief Joe Pignatelli Teaching Video Portion of Annual Bail Out Drill

Connor Raymond, Dimetrio Martinez

Julian Pettiford, Brett Politi

Our Department on Fire & Rescue Calls

Before the Patterson Fire Department was formed there was little help fighting fires in town. The nearest fire departments were in Brewster and Carmel. The Townsend & Pendleton Sash Factory, which was located near the railroad, had a hand drawn pumping engine which was brought to help fight some fires. On April 5, 1902, a huge fire destroyed the Townsend & Pendleton factory and most of the businesses near the railroad. The first two pictures below are the aftermath of that fire. This section contains photographs of fires and rescue operations conducted by the Patterson Fire Department over the past 100 years.

Juilus Pahlch Jr., Richard Tompkins, Bobby Bubenicek, John Covell, Gerald Butler, Caleb Smith Sr.

Fire at PhilBeth's Store & Repair Shop on Front Street

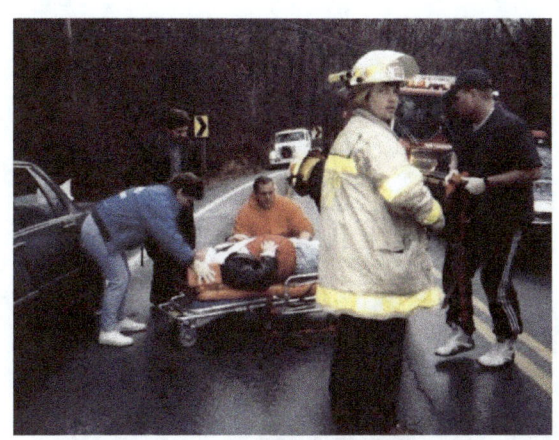

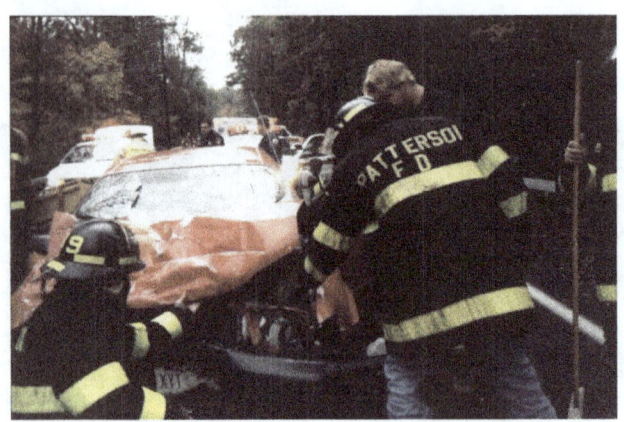

102

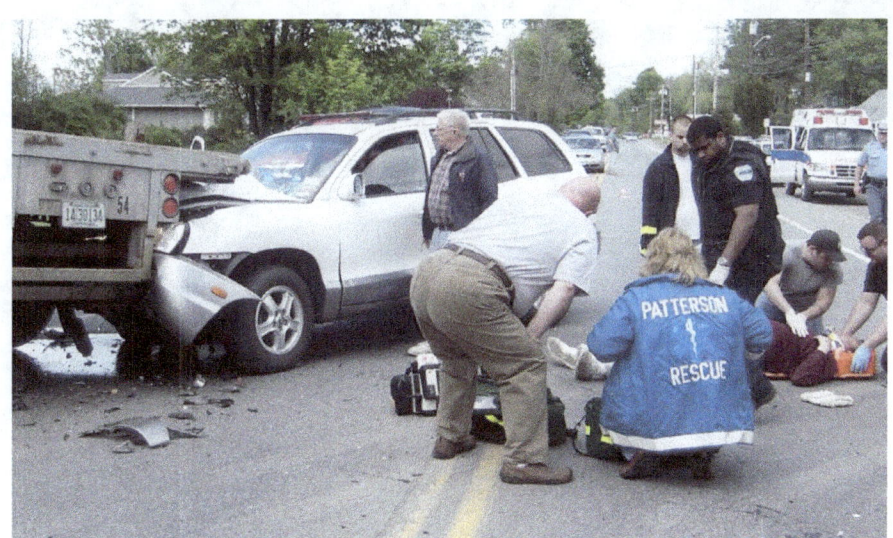

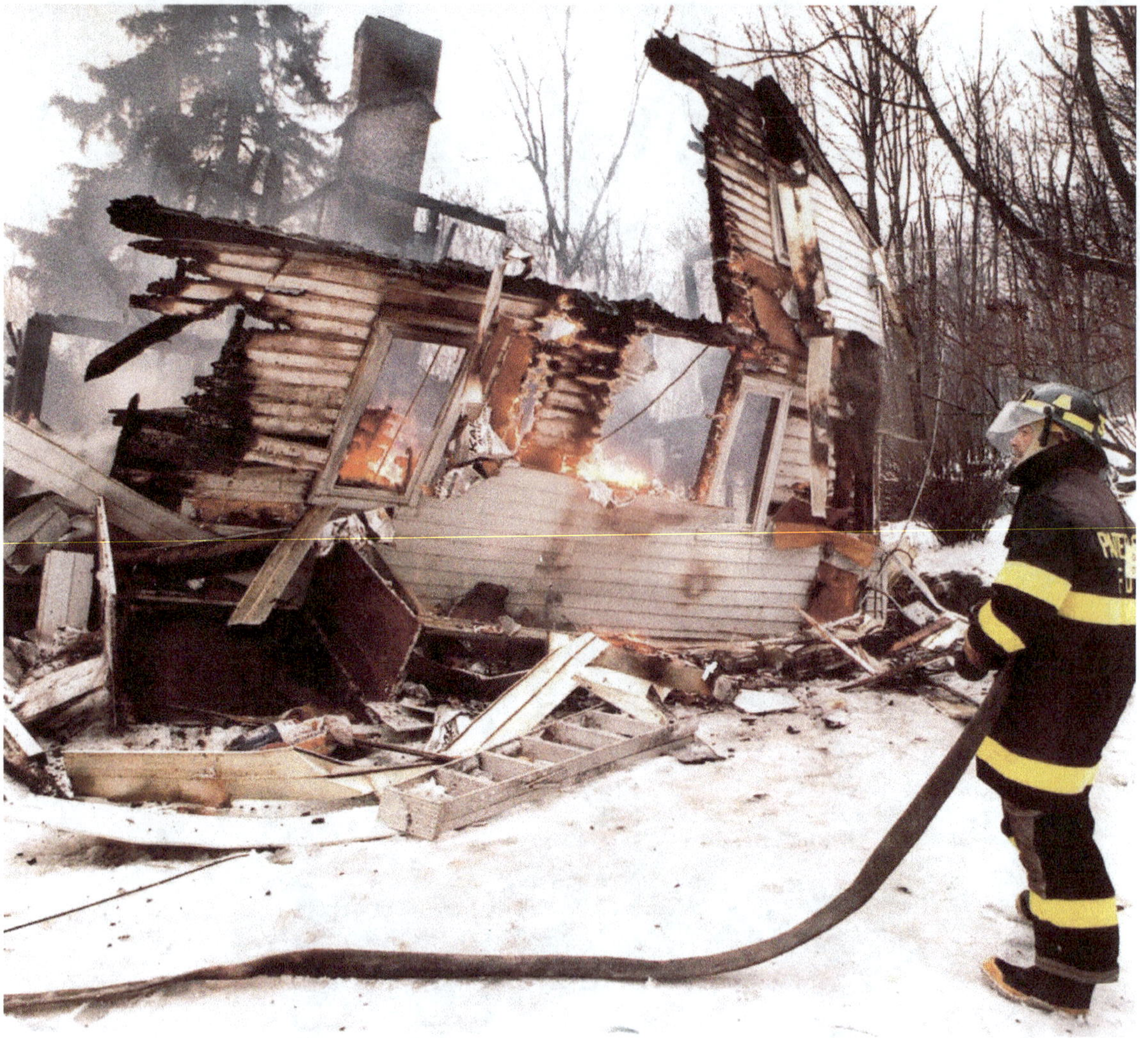

FIRE POLICE
FIRE POLICE
FIRE POLICE
KVD © 2010

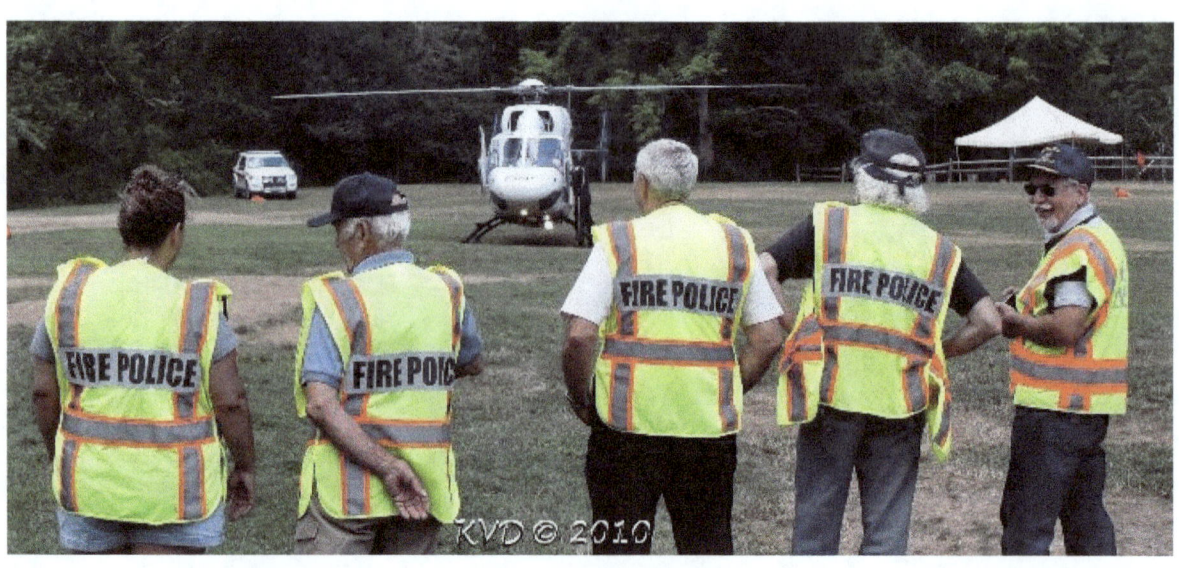

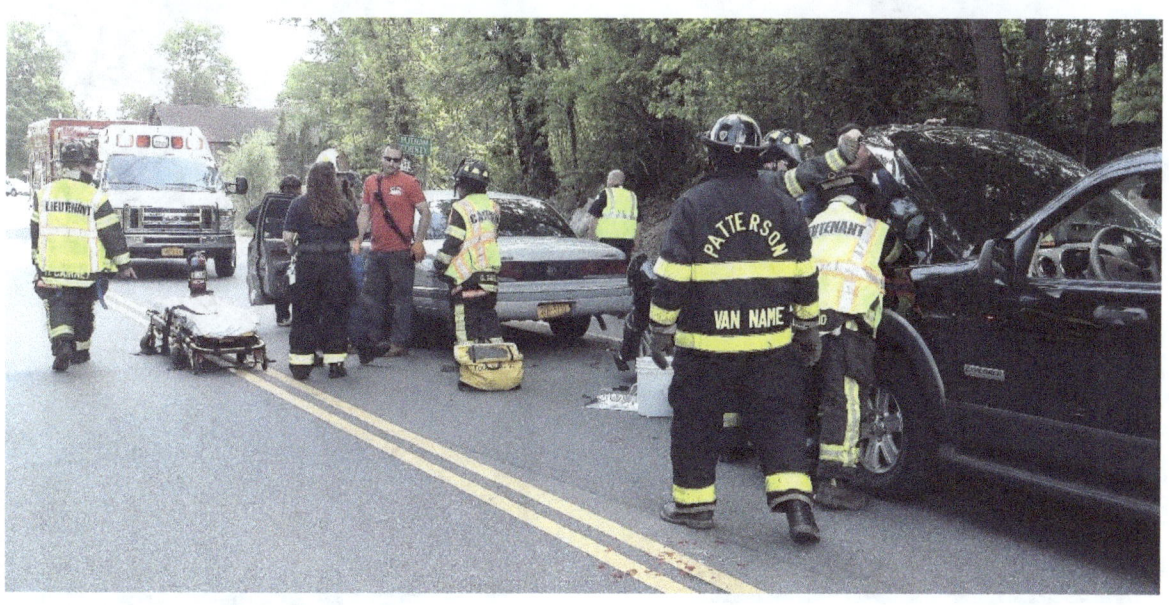

Albert Rossi

Joe Pignatelli, Randall Mulkins, Jesse Greco, Danielle French

Our Members in Parades

Throughout our history our department has participated in many parades. Most years we do a Memorial Day parade in town. We usually host a Fire Parade each year where fire departments from surrounding areas participate. Those are juried parades with trophies awarded in various categories. We also participate in many fire parades in other towns.

George Gronke & Emil Renak Holding Banner.

Emil Renak, Bobby Smith Sr., Charles Van Keuren, George Buechal, Gerald Baker, Jimmy Tence, George Apap, Marty Kessman, Bobby Bubenicek

Former Chiefs William Bubenicek Sr. and Donald Smith, James Rinaldi Sr. driving.

John Covall, Charlie Smyth, Brian Burdick, John Brugger, Bob Bell, Lois Covell Ward, Pat O'Connell, Kevin O'Connell, Lee Conway

Raena Gallagher, Beverly Lauro, Mary O'Connel, Jessie Cole

Steve Colt, Lois Covell Ward, Frank Brunow, Pat O'Connell, Paul Piazza Sr., Rusty Mulkins, Bob Lauro, John Covell

Loretta Kennedy, Lois Covell Ward, Bob Smith Jr., Adam Stiebeling, John Deitz, Andrew Weise, Jesse Gonzalez, Ann Darow, Chris Van Name, Stavos

Russel Mulkins, Bobby Smith Jr., George Banks, Bob Bell, Lee Conway, Matt Kelly, Glen Baker

Paul Greenwood, Lee Conway, Mike O'Connell, P.J. O'Connell, Russ Shay, Steve Colt

Steve Colt, Brian Vigliotti, Tommy Lee, Sean Fredericks, Mike Covell

Brian Burdick, Paul Smith, Matt Kelly, Mike Smyth, Kevin Butler, Timmy Smith, Frank Smith, Richard Graham, Eleanora Smith, Paul Piazza Sr., Bob Lauro, T.C. Covell, P.J. O'Connell

Steve Colt, Bob Lauro, Ray Poletta, Adam Stiebeling, Paul Piazza, George Banks, Frank Smith, John Covell, Russell Mulkins

Jesse Gonzalez, Russel Mulkins, Vinny Montouro, Sheri Citrone

Paul Smith, Kyle Lyons, Connor Raymond, Tommy Gamache, Cody Hickok, Albert Rossi

Activities With Our Department

Over the years the Patterson Fire Department conducted numerous activities for the department and the community. Some events included picnics, dances, festivals, penny socials, fishing derbies, clam bakes, winter carnivals, and turkey, chicken & goose shoots. The department conducted Memorial Day parades and services and more recently 9-11 Memorials. Carnivals have been an annual event for many years. Some were followed by dazzling fireworks. The department provides Fire Prevention programs to area schools. During World War II the department conducted a War Fund Drive. Some more recent events included holiday tree lighting, children's Christmas party, candy cane run with Santa, car shows, book sales, and family fun days.

John Carey, Gus Birch, Scott Eastwood & David V. Smith at Fishing Derby

Founding Member Rev. Horace Hillery (2nd from Left) and Others

Don Smith, George Apap, Bob Smith Sr., Willie Boone, Martin Kessman

Nancy Farrell

Pat O'Connell, Randy Mulkins, Loretta Kennedy

Carol Smith, Cindy Covell, Irene Covell, Lee Conway

Tommy Lee Received Trophy for Department

Bill & Gail Hoshspring

John Radtke, Bob Johnson, Lynn Andretta, Paul & Eileen Ciatto, Andy Andretta,
Cindy & John Covell, Henry Brunow, Nick Comatas

Fire Prevention

Lt. John Bodor Fire Prevention

Vinny Montouro Fire Prevention

Bob Bell & Fire Prevention Helpers

Diane Vishinski Fire Prevention

Annual Carnival

Easter Egg Hunt

Paul Maass, Del Goldsmith

Halloween Costume Party

Firefighters Ski Competition at Thunder Ridge

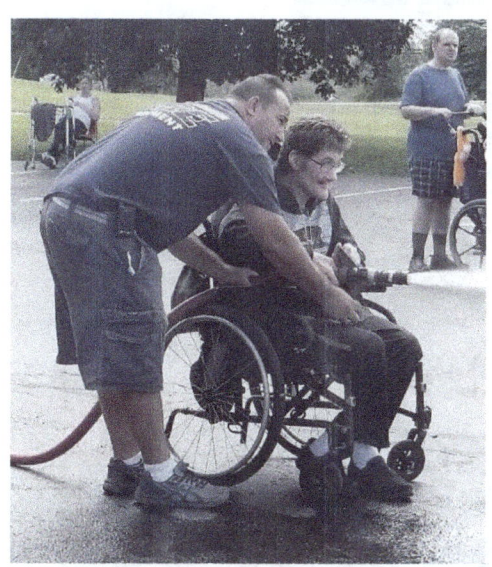
Vinny Montouro

P. Piazza, A. Stiebeling, J. Fredericks, T. Lee, C. Brown

Eleanora Smith, Tommy Gamache, Raul Vielman, Tim Stottle, John Bodor, Tammy Smith, Frank Smith, Bob Cuomo, Debbie Miller, Eileen & Charile Smyth, Henry Brunow, Joe Pignatelli, Tim Perrault, Ed Centofante, Kae Oakley, Randall Mulkins, Tony Oakley, Ann Daros, T.J. & Loretta Kennedy, Bob Miller, Zachary Mulkins

Del & Ann Goldsmith, Bob Lauro Pat O'Connell

Connor Raymond, Joe Pignatelli, Ricky Medina, Andrew Rossi, Santa T., Brandy Telesco, Albert Rossi

9-11 Remembrance Services

Car Show

Relay for Life

Paint the Town Purple for Relay for Life

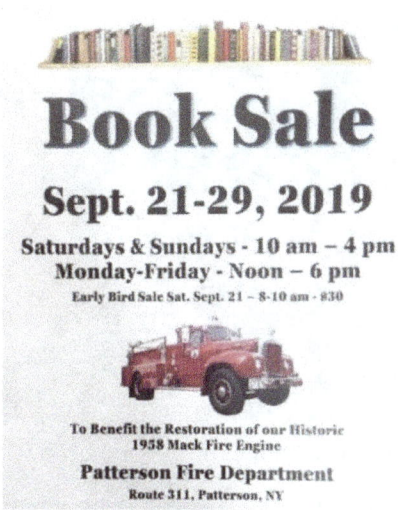

Larry Maxwell & Mario Gabrielli at Book Sale

Book Sale Under the Pavilion

John Barretto

Randall Mulkins at Relay for Life

Violet, Larry & Robert Maxwell
Santa Montana

Albert Rossi, Cody Hickox, Andrew Aiken, John Barretto, Joe Pignatelli, Justin Shepps

Scott Miller, Joe Nickischer, Andrew Aiken, John Barretto, Andrew Rossi, Ed O'Connell, Connor Raymond, Albert Rossi

Our Members Over the Years

This section contains a variety of photographs of our members, associate members, and auxiliary members over the past 100 years.

Some of Our Original Members
Most of These Photos Are When They Were Older

Jacob Block

John Carey

Abel Davis

Junia Dykeman

Howard Kelley

Howard Knapp

George Pfahl

George Robinson

David V. Smith

Ernest Tompkins

Dr. Albert Towner

Paul Townsend

Members in Front of the Old Station 1926-1931 – Henry Ludington & Junia Dykeman in Center in White Hats. Daniel Ludington Front Row Left.

Members of Pumper Company on our 1937 Mack in Front of Our Old Station
Picture Taken September 1937

Members on 1937 Mack in September 1937. All Shown Below in Expanded Images

Junia W. Dykeman, Jr.

William J. Bubenicek, Sr.

Francis "Frank" Leyden, Sr.

Clarence Sprague

Ferris J. Sprague, Sr.

John Carey

Henry S. Ludington, Sr.

Burton Twin

Frank Grady

Daniel G. Ludington

Burton Twin

Members from Patterson Fire Department at Special Service
Frank Brunow Sr., Francis Lyden Jr., Rev. Horace Hillery, Tommy Bubenicek,
Johnny Van Keuran, Bob Millar, Donald Smith, Frank Grady & members from other departments

Images of Members Captured from the 1960 Film "Our Town"

Donald B. Smith

Lorne Covell

Roy Covell

John Sprague

Harry Freeman

Neal Lacey, Jr.

Frank Grady, Sr.

Kenny Renak

Johnny Van Keuren

Steve "Red" Awryitis

Kent Nicola

Jimmy Tence

Lars Petersen, Kit Petersen, Mike Colt, Johnny Van Keuren, Wally Parent, Charles Van Keuren, Bob Dwyer, Thomas McLaughlin, William Bubenicek Sr., Fred Buechel, George Buechel, Emil Renak Francis Lyden Jr., Tommy Bubenicek, Rev. Horace Hillery, Bill Millar, Donald Smith

Richard Tompkins, Bud Sprague, Ernie Lee, Martin Kessman, Spencer Harby, George Pfahl William Bubenicek Sr., Gerald Baker, Caleb Smith Sr., Bobby Smith Sr., Bobby Bubenicek, Tom Malone, Ferris Sprague, Jimmy Rinaldi Jr., Tommy Brandon, Hollis Baker, William Bubenicek Jr.

Gerald Baker, Caleb Smith Sr., Don Smith, Wm. Bubenicek, Sr. and Jimmy Rinaldi Sr.

Emil Buechel, Wm. Bubenicek Sr., Don Smith, George Pfahl, Kenny Renak, Bob Smith Sr., Gerald Baker, Caleb Smith Sr., Rev. Hillery, Wm. Bubenicek Jr., Del Goldsmith, Charles Van Keuren

Tommy McDougal and Don Smith in Center

Herb Schneck, Russ Shay, Tom Paschal

Roger Tricinelli, Caleb Smith Sr.

Jimmy Fredericks, Harry Bryant, Wally Perrant, John Radtke, Del Goldsmith, Joe Brunow, Jimmy Rinaldi Sr., Charles Van Keruran, John Covell, Frank Brunow, Roger Tricinelli, Lorne Covell, Harold Cole, Greg Petersen, Kenny Renak, Hollis Baker, Marty Kessman, Mike Colt, Rev. James Frost, Paul Agar, Bill Gronke, Teddy Covell, Francis Lyden, Willie Boone, Richard Tompkins, Tony Boone, George Pfhal, John Bodor

Richard Tompkins, Gerald Baker, Willie Boone, Don Smith

Russ Shay, Barry Harney, John Covell, Tommy Lee, Alfred Truesdal, Steve Colt, Walt Sprague, Walt McCekron, Spencer Harby, Jimmy Rinaldi, Bill Gronke, Rev. James Frost, Jim Tence, Bobby Poligi, Marie Gronke, Julia Boone, Trudy Mill, Rose Perrin, Harry Bryant, Roger Tricinelli

Matt Kelly, Adam Stiebeling, Lee Conway, John Covell, Bob Bell, Thomas Florio, T. Lee, Bob Lauro, Donna Hazzard, Chris Murray, Nancy Hammond

Tony Oakley, Brian Yates, Andrew Rossi, Mario Gabrielli, Albert Rossi, Eleanora Smith, John Covell, Russell Mulkins, Debbie Miller

Bob Bell, Bob Smith Sr., Lee Conway, George Banks, Bob Lauro, Trudy Mill, Beverly Lauro, Joe Ciatto

Adam Stiebeling, Frank Brunow Sr., George Banks, Ray Poletta, Jim Fredericks, John Covell, Angie McGoorty, Bob Smith Jr., Frank Smith. Cindy Covell, Lars Petersen, Bob Bell, Lee Conway, Paul Piazza Sr., Henry Brunow, Bobby Johnson, Paul Piazza Jr., Tracy Smith, Ed Centofante, Lois Covell Ward, Tiffany Martin, Diane Vishinski, Al Hudson, Jim Fredericks, George Banks, Billy Cole

Mike O'Connell, Bob Smith Sr., Bill Hochspring, Bobby Bubenicek, Chuck Romeo, John Radtke

Jim Lowe, Jimmy Fredericks, Ray Poletta, Angie McGoorty, Bob Bell, Eleanora Smith, Mike Covell, Bob Smith Jr., Paul Piazza, Adam Steibleing, Bob Johnson, Brian Burdick, Timmy Smith

Wilson Cajas, Cody Hickok, John Barretto, Albert Rossi, Randall Mulkins, Andrew Rossi

John Covell, Matt Kelly, Louis Chamberlain

Ernie Lee, Bud Dwyer

Chuck Bostick, Brian Burdick, Eleanora Smith, Pat O'Connell, Bobby Smith Jr., Ed Farrell

Santa Castellano, John Barretto

Hollis Baker, Bud Dwyer, Emil Renak

Tommy "Doc" Lee, Lee Conway, George "Put" Banks, Paul Smith, Some Brewster Members

Tom Dixon, Tony Oakley, Ed O'Conner, John Deitz, Sheri Citrone, Chris Deitz

Ed Centofante, Mike Semo, Willie & Julia Boone, Roger Tricinelli

Mike Semo, Paul Smith, Monica Defoe, Ann Denholm, Rick Bosser, Arturo Jara.
Angie McGoorty, Eleanora Smith, Larry Maxwell

Russell Shay, Mary O'Connell, Al Hudson

J. Covell, B. Johnson, P. Piazza, P. Smith. L. Kennedy

Tom Dixon, Chris Deitz, Kurt Vondietsch, Karl Brenner, Dave Orifici, Brian Vigliotti

Tom Pasko

Randy Mulkins, Tommy "Doc" Lee

Glen Baker, Charlie Smyth, Paul Smith, George Apap, Ed Farrell, Randall Mulkins, Diane Vishinski, Henry Brunow, Bob Bell, Mike Semo

Frank Brunow, Frank Farrell, Louis Chamberlian, Mike Semo, Charlie Smyth, Del Goldsmith, John Bodor, Ed Centofante, Nelson Barrett, Frank Grady, Bob Bondi, Dick Armstead

Eleanora Smith, Henry Brunow Sr., Burt Gonci, Louis Chamberlain, Stan Vishinski, Bob Lauro, Paul Maass, Angie McGoorty, Brian Burdick, Tonianne Bourke, Timmy Smith, Willis Stephens Jr.

Brian Burdick, Diane Vishinski, Matt Szpindor, Jim Fredericks, Rich Bosser, Bob Johnson

Bob Bell, Rich Bosser, Jim Fredericks, Caleb Frank Smith, Brian Burdick, Lois Covell Ward, Chris Deitz, Tommy Lee, John Deitz, Tom Dixon, Dale Brown, Paul Maass, John Bodor, Chris Lomedico, Raul Vielman, Brian Vigliotti, Tony Oakley, Ray Poletta

Albert Rossi, Arturo Jara, Larry Maxwell, Tommy Gamache. Joe Pignatelli, Loretta Kennedy, Wilson Cajas, Rich Bosser, John Barretto, Andrew Aiken, John Deitz, Zachary Mulkins, Randall Mulkins

Bob Smith Jr., Jimmy Frederick, , Billy Cole, Henry Brunow, Steve Colt

Eileen & Joe Ciatto, Lynn & Andy Andretta and Mary & Pat O'Connell

Herb & Irene Schech, Charlie & Eileen Smyth and Sharon & Rick Olsen

Bob & Carol Smith, Paul Smith, Al Truesdal, Paul & Shirley Agar, Walter Sprague, Lisa Barbaritta

Spence & Carrie Harby, Calvin & Date, Willie & Julia Boone, Terry & Danny Schutz and Tom & Sis Krepil

Russ & Joyce Shay, Franke & Kathy Farrell, Eileen & Joe Ciatto & Linda Antunnuci, Eileen & Charlie Smyth

Pat & Mary O'Connell, Cherly Pegano & Date, Carol Sherwood, Tom & B. Bubenicek and Ro & Wally Perrin

Paul & Judi Piaza, Nick & Wife Dougherty, Herman & Merle Weber, Debbie & Mike Piazza, Tom Kerpil

Bob Bell, Pattie Greenwood, Billy & K. Smith, Jim & Pam Tence, Bill & Pat Brown and Irene & H. Schech

Lorne & Esther Covell, Pete & Bonne McEckron, Ronald & Anna Maynard, Fred Beuchel

Lars Petersen, Pat O'Connell, John Radke, Paul Agar Bi, lly Smith

Joan & B. Costello, Lucy & B. Bubenieck, Ann & M. Montesano, Rosina & L. Petersen and Ellen & M. Walsh

John Radtke, Buzzy & Lucy Buzzutto, Joan & Bobby Costello, Ro Perrin, Anne & Michale Montesano

Spencer & Carrie Harby and Julia & Willie Boone

Bev & Bob Lauro, Ed & Cathy Farrell and Guests

Bob Johnson, Curt Wargo, John Covell

Pat O'Connell, Andy Andretta, Joe Ciatto

Ed Centofante, Nelson Barrett, Del Goldsmith, John Bodor, George Banks,
P.J. O'Connell, Roger St. Martins

Larry Lawlor, Bob Smith Sr., John Covell, Bob Lauro

Larry Lawlor, Herb Scheck, Lars Petersen
Eileen Smyth, J. Radtke, John Baker, P. Piazza Sr.

Diane Vishinski, Herb Scheck, Bob Bell,
John Radtke, Russ. Shay, Bob Laurel

Larry Lawlor, Curt Wargo, Bob Bell, Pat O'Connell

Herman Weber, Pat O'Connell, Anne Wargo
Lynn Andretta, Cindy Covell, Mike Semo

Larry Lawlor, Ed Centofante, George Apap
Del Goldsmith, John Bodor, Tom Pasko

A. Steibling, D. Goldsmith, P.J. O'Connell

Anne Wargo, Lynn Andretta, Eileen Smyth, Irene Scheck

Lee Conway, R. Mulkins, B. Smith, H. Brunow

P.J. O'Connell, George Banks, Russell Mulkins

Tommy Bubenicek

Cindy Covell, Patricia Greenwood

Bob Bell

Richard Lyden

Curt Wargo

John Baker, Guest, P. J. O'Connell

Tommy Bubenicek, Bobby Costello

Station 1 Captain Bob Bell & Captain of Station 2

Richard Lyden, Bobby Johnson

Eileen & Charlie Smyth

Bob Johnson, Don Smith

Russ Shay, John Bruger

Russell Mulkins, Frank Farrell, Ed O'Connell

Andrew & Albert Rossi

Tom & Bridget Pasko, Phil Porcelli

Bob Cuomo

Willie & Julia Boone

Marlene Fisher, Donna Hazzard, Ann Johnson
Mary O'Connell, Theresa & Tina Williams

Curt Wargo

  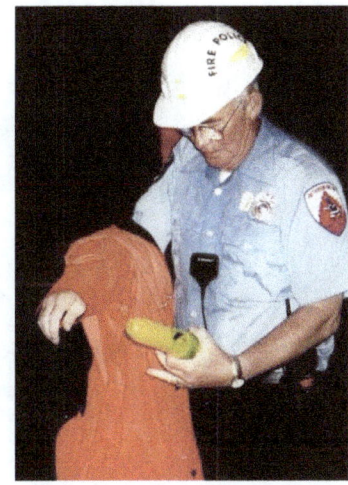

| Lee Chamberlain | Pat O'Connell | Ed Farrell |

| Joe & Jeremy Tompkins | Andrew & Albert Rossi | Matt & Justin Szpindor |

| Paul Piazza | Cody Hickok | Adam Stiebeling |

Cindy Covell

Angie McGoorty, Ann Denholm

Matt Szpindor, Andrew Kroger, Andrew Rossi, Ricky Medina, Justin Szpindor, Albert Rossi, Randall Mulkins, Tim Perrault, Zachary Mulkins

Glen Baker, Ed Farrell, Kevin Butler, Russell Mulkins

Timmy Smith

Herb Schech

Pat O'Connell

Brian Burdick, Dave Lanek, Ray Poletta, Eleanora Smith. Tim Smith. Bobby Smith Jr., Bob Johnson, Adam Stiebeling, Frank Smith Jr, Jimmy Fredericks, Paul Piazza Jr, Paul Piazza Sr.

Ann & Del Goldsmith

Paul Agar

Instructor, Tom Dixon, Kurt Vondietsch, Eleanora Smith, Sheri Citrone, Joey Nickisher, Derick Maurice, John Bodor

Ann Daros, Chris Van Name, John Bodor, Matt Szpindor, Raul Vielman, Frank Smith, Eleanora Smith, Adam Stiebeling, Ed Centofante, Charlie & Eileen Smyth, Paul Maass, Chris Deitz, Justin Shepps

John Bodor, Ed Centafanni, Paul Smith. Paul Maass, John Covell, Rick Cable, Robert Smith Jr., Chris Brown, Adam Stiebeling, Phil Porcelli, Del Goldsmith

John Covell, Brian Burdick, Timmy Smith, Tonianne Bourke, President Bill Clinton, Sen. Hillary Clinton, Face removed of person who asked not to be identified, Bert Gonci, Mike Covell

Colleen Brown, Beverly Lauro, Mary O'Connell
Linda Griffin, Santa & Bob Johnson

Guest, Curt Wargo, Putnam Co.Exec. David Bruen

E. Smith, Adam Stiebeling, Bob Laurel, Ray Paletta, Monica & Ben Shavone, Frank Smith

Henry Brunow, Mike Covell

Ray Paletta, Brian Burdick, Sheri Citrone

Brian Vigliotti, Caleb Frank Smith III　　　　　　Raul Vielman

Rich Tompkins, Jimmy Tence, Willie Boone

Eleanora Smith　　　　　　Kyle Fredericks, Brandy Telesco, Vinny Montouro

Ed Centofante, Charlie Smyth, Louis Chamberlain, Angie McGoorty, Frank Brunow Sr., Ed Farrell, Larry Mendel, Stan Vishinski, John Radtke

Paul Maass

Tommy Gamache, Steve Keck

Tom Florio, Adam Steibeling, Matt Kelly, John Covell, Eleanora Smith, Lee Conway, Bob Lauro

Timmy Smith, Sean Fredericks, Jimmy Fredericks, Keck, John Bodor, Justin Shepps, Chris Deitz, Kurt Vondietsch

Mike Semo   Matt Castellano, Chris Van Name   Andrew Rossi

E. & P. Smith, R. Montana, J. Pignatelli, V. Montouro, A. Stiebeling

Joe Doceti, JoePignatelli, Ryan Forrester, Steve Keck, Roy Forrester, Brandy Telesco, Kyle Fredericks, Ann Daros, Monica Defoe, Ron Schultz, Eleanora Smith

Phil Porcelli, Paul Mass, Dale Brown

John Simpson

John Bodor, Ed Centofante

Stacie Spinney, Paul & Lois Maass

Ricky Montana, Brandy Telesco, Steve Keck   Joe Montana, Andrew Aiken, Zachary Mulkins

Albert Rossi   Dimetrio Martinez   Wilson Cajas

Angie McGoorty, Bob Johnson, Ed Centaofante   Arturo Jara, Seri Citrone, Diane Vishinski
Phil Porcelli

Larry Maxwell, Arturo Jara, John Simpson, Brian Yates

Brandon Pocali, Ricky Medina, Adam Kroger

Vinny Montouro , Stavos

Justin & Matt Szpindor, Tony Lopez, Andrew Rossi

Albert Rossi, Joe Montana, Santa Terwilliger, Andrew Rossi, Randall Mulkins

Ricky Montana, Kae Oakley, Brandy Telesco ,Sean Fredericks

Joe Pignatelli

Larry Maxwell, Rich Bosser, Vinny Montouro, Andrew Rossi, Joe Nickischer, Paul Smith, Justin Szpindor, Tommy Gamache, Kyle Fredericks, Matt Szpindor, Connor Raymond, Tim Perrault, Albert Rossi, Ann Denholm, Eleanora Smith

Connor Raymond

Chris Deitz, Steve Colt, Henry Brunow

Jesse Greco, Joe Pignatelli, John Deitz

Joe Nickischer, Chris Van Name, Andrew Rossi, Russell Mulkins, Andrew Aiken

Larry Maxwell, Albert Rossi, Sean Terwilliger, Albert Rossi, Matt Szpindor, Tommy Gamache
Raul Vielman, Wlison Cajas, John Barretto

Albert Rossi & Sean Fredericks

Bob Bell III, Ray Poletta, Paul Piazza, Brian Burdick

Justin Szpindor, Albert Rossi, Connor Raymond, Brandy Telesco

Arturo Jara, John Simpson, Phil Porcelli, Mike Semo, Ricky Montana, Albert Rossi, Mario Gabrielli, Brandy Telesco, Eileen Smyth, Raul Vielman, Charlie Smyth, Brian Yates, Larry Maxwell, Susan Goldsmith, Ed Centofante, Debbie Miller, Vinny Montouro

Mario Gabrielli, Joe Pignatelli, Connor Raymond, John Barretto

Brandy Telesco, Randall Mulkins, Jesse Greco, John Barretto

"The Boys"

Raul Vielman Becomes a U.S. Citizen

Donating a Bicycle to Accident Victim During Covid Pandemic
Patterson Ambulance & Patterson Fire Department
Larry Maxwell, Denise Montana, Tommy Gamache, John Barretto, Connor Raymond, Joe Pignatelli
Jesse Ventura, Family Receiving Bicycle in Front Row

Alex Amendoeira, Connor Raymond, Jesse Greco, Randall Mulkins, Danielle French

Our Corporate Officers 2021

President Randall Mulkins, Vice President Andrew Aikens, Recording Secretary Loretta Kennedy, Corresponding Secretary Zachary Mulkins, Treasurer Arturo Jara, Trustee Wilson Cajas, Trustee Richard Bosser, Trustee John Barretto

Our Firematic Officers 2021

Captain Station 2 Chris Deitz, Captain Station 1 Albert Rossi , Chaplain Larry A. Maxwell, 2nd Asst. Chief John Deitz, 1st Asst. Chief Joe Pignatell, Chief Tommy Gamache

Our Officers, Lieutenants & Foremen 2021

Mario Gabrielli, Brandy Telesco, Chris Deitz, Randall Mulkins, Albert Rossi, Larry Maxwell, Loretta Kennedy, John Deitz, Wlison Cajas, Joe Pignatelli, Raul Vielman, Tommy Gamache

Ladder Truck Company 2021

Mario Gabrielli, Zachary Mulkins, Andrew Aiken, Joe Montana, Danielle French

Heavy Rescue Company 2021

Wilson Cajas, Jim Lowe, Raul Vielman, Brett Politi

Engine Company 2021

Andrew Rossi, John Barretto, Matt Castellano

Tanker Company 2021

Jesse Greco, Randall Mulkins

Ambulance Company 2021

Larry Maxwell, John Simpson, Albert Rossi. Randall Mulkins, James Dipietrantonio, Henry Brunow, Loretta Kennedy, Brandy Telesco, Raul Vielman, Mario Gabrielli

Station Two Company 2021

James Dipietrantonio, Tim Perault, Justin Sheeps
Adam Stiebleling, Connor Raymond

Station 2 Captain
Chris Deitz

Fire Police Company 2021

Larry Maxwell, John Simpson, Arturo Jara, Henry Brunow, Ann Denholm, Dimetrio Martinez, Loretta Kennedy, Carol Porcali, Angie McGoorty, Ed Centofante, Lt. Phil Porcelli

Women's Auxiliary 2021

Marlene Green Fisher, Bridget Pasko, Ann Montesano, Kae Oakley, Margaret Kessman, Mary Bodor, Trudy Mill, Rosina "Tootsie" Petersen, Stacie Spinney

Associate Members 2021

Sue Bouton, Susan Goldsmth, Debbie Miller, Robert Miller

Our Presidents

When the Patterson Fire Department was organized in 1921, the Captain ran the business meetings. In 1930, the office of President was established. The President became the chief corporate officer for the Fire Department and served as Chairman for the meetings. We were unable to locate photographs for 3 of our past presidents, all 3 were veterans..

Junia W. Dykeman, Jr.
1930-1932

Newton K. McNeil
1932-1934

Dr. Albert N. Towner
1934-1936

David V. Smith
1936-1939

Daniel G. Ludington
1939-1940

R. Fred Wood
1940-1941

Michael C. Burns
1941-1943

Francis W. Lyden, Sr.
1943-1946

George F. Pulling
1946-1948

William J. Bubenicek, Sr.
1948-1953

Charles H. Van Keuren
1953-54, 1957-1960's, 1968

Charles T. Hampe
1954-1955

William Millar
1955-1957

James Rinaldi, Sr.
Mid 1960's

George McCekron
Before 1968

Paul Agar
1970-1972

Erik "Lars" Petersen
1972-1974

John Radtke
1974-1975, 1979-1981

William Smith, Jr.
1975-1977

Patrick L. O'Connell
1977-1979

Herb Schech
1981-1989, 1991-1992

Charles Smyth
1989-1991, 1998-2000

Robert Bell, Jr.
1992-1995

Henry Brunow
1995-1998

Caleb Franklin Smith III
2000-2007

Brian Burdick
2007-2008

Paul Smith
2008-2011

Eleanora Smith
2011-2018

Mario Gabrielli
2018-2021

Randall Mulkins
2021- Present

Our Chiefs

Our First Three Captains
(Before Office of Chief)

Dr. Reed F. Haviland
Apr. 26, 1921 – July 6, 1921

Mortimer B. Townsend
Sep. 7, 1921-May 1, 1922

Henry S. Ludington
May 1, 1922-May 5, 1930

Our Chiefs
The office of Chief was established in our department in May 1930.

Henry S. Ludington
1930–1931

Junia W. Dykeman, Sr.
1931-1941

William J. Bubenicek, Sr.
1941-1945

Ferris J. Sprague
1945-1954

Donald B. Smith
1954-1963

Thomas G. MacDougal
1963-1965

William J. Bubenicek
1965-1968

Robert Smith, Sr.
1968-1970

Willie C. Boone, Jr.
1970-1973

Rev. James Frost
1973-1974

James Tence
1974-1976

Roger Tricenelli
1976-1977

John Covell, Jr.
1977-1987, 1989-1991

John Brugger
1978-1979

Robert Johnson
1979-1981

Curt Wargo
1981-1982

Robert Bell
1983-1985

Patrick L. O'Connell
1985-1987

Andrew Andretta
1987-1989

Paul Piazza, Sr.
1990-1991

Lee Conway
1991-1993, 1997-2000

Russell A. Mulkins
1993-1996, 2004-2005

George Banks
1996-1997

Adam Stiebeling
2000-2003, 2011-2012

Robert Smith, Jr.
2003-2004

Caleb Franklin Smith III
2006–2011

Ed O'Connell
2011

Matthew Szpindor
2012-2019

Joseph Nichersher
2019-2020

Tommy Gamache
2020-Present

Honorary Chief
Edward "Ed" Centofante

Our department bestowed the honor of Honorary Chief on Edward "Ed "Centofante. Ed joined the Department in the 1974. He became part of the new Fire Police Team headed by Lieutenant John Bodor.

Ed served in the United States Navy in World War II. He was only 17 years old when he enlisted, so he needed special permission, and he had to agree to serve until the end of the war. He served both in the Atlantic and Pacific.

After the war, Ed became a builder. He built thousands of homes on Long Island.

He and his wife Marie, their son, and two daughters moved to Patterson, New York in 1974.

In 1991, when Charlie Smyth was President of the Fire Department, Ed helped build the new fire station on Burdick Road. He also helped build the Station Two on Bullet Hole Road.

Even at age 96, Ed remains active as a Fire Police Officer in the Patterson Fire Department.

Our Chaplains

At the annual meeting of the department, on May 2, 1927, minutes show the election of the departments first official Chaplain, Rev. Horace H. Hillery. Over the years some laymen were appointed Deputy Chaplains. Only a few members were elected as Chaplains. Of the elected Chaplains, four were ordained ministers who served as pastors of churches in town, two layman who were elected chaplain, one was of the Jewish faith. In New York State elected Chaplains are firematic officers. Their rank is the same as a chief.

Rev. Henry F. Watts

The Rev. H. F. Watts was one of the founding members of the Patterson Fire Department in 1921. He served as the Pastor of the Patterson Presbyterian Church. Though official records do not show him bearing the title Chaplain, it was customary for organizations back then to have ordained clergy fulfill duties which would later be relegated to the office of Chaplain. Rev. Watts served in the department until he moved away in 1923.

Rev. Horace E. Hillery

The Rev. Horace E. Hillery was the first person officially elected to serve as chaplain for the department on May 2, 1927. He joined the department in 1926. He served as the Pastor of the Patterson Presbyterian Church from 1923 to 1951. After he retired from the church he became the first Putnam County Historian in 1953.

Rev. George Beimler

The Rev. George Beimler was elected Chaplain of the department in 1958. He served as the Pastor of the Patterson Presbyterian Church from 1952 through 1962.

S. Delvalle "Del" Goldsmith

From 1955 to 2000 S. Delvalle "Del" Goldsmith served the Patterson Fire Department as a firefighter then as a Fire Police Officer. He was a layman of the Jewish faith, who became Chaplain in 1971. He served in that role numerous times. He served as an Acting President and as Vice President. He also served as a chaplain for the Putnam Northern Westchester Fire Police Association. In 2006, the third Firehouse of the Patterson Fire Department was named in his honor. He was honored by the department as Chaplain Emeritus.

Rev. James B. M. Frost

The Rev. James B. M. Frost, Sr. served the Fire Department in various roles. He was a firefighter and served as Chief and as Chaplain. He was elected Chaplain in 1974. He served in that role, alternating with Del Goldsmith a number of times. He served as the of the Presbyterian Church from 1966 to 1990, when he retired. He was honored by the department as Chaplain Emeritus.

Paul C. Maass

Paul C. Maass was a Volunteer firefighter with the Kent Fire Department before moving to Patterson. When he came to Patterson he became an interior firefighter. He then became a Fire Police Officer. He was a layman who served as Chaplain. He served until his death in 2016. He was an avid musician.

Rev. Dr. Larry A. Maxwell

In 2016, the Rev. Dr. Larry A. Maxwell was appointed Deputy-Chaplain of the Department. He was then elected Chaplain in 2017. He is also a Fire Police Officer and Emergency Medical Technician (EMT). He is a member of the New York State Fire Chaplains Association and a Chaplain for the Northern Westchester Fire Police Association. He represents our department and conducts firematic funeral service for fire departments throughout Dutchess, Putnam and Westchester Counties. He became Pastor of the Patterson Baptist Church in 1995 and currently serves there. He is the Town of Patterson Historian.

Members Who Served in the Military

Spanish American War

Kenneth Hall

World War I

Hjalmar Anderson	Howard E. Knapp	Paul W. Townsend
Gordon Eastwood	Newton K. McNeill	Rev. Henry F. Watts
John F. Eastwood	Albert N. Towner	
Howard E. Kelley	Clarence Smith	

World War II

Gerald A. Baker	George Flint	Lawrence Scapporretta
Howard Booth	Francis G. Gaydos	Warren M. Scapperotta
Robert M. Bubenicek	Charles T. Hampe	John Scheck
Thomas J. Bubenicek	Richard Harrison	Charles H. Van Keuren
William J. Bubenicek	Reid L. Haviland	Joseph Van Keuren
Edward Centofante	George Flint	R. Fred Ward
Francis R. Brunow	Ernest Lee	John Widman, Jr.
Mortimer G. Carey	Francis W. Leyden, Jr.	Wilbert Widman
Francis "Zeke" Drnek	Douglas Mackey	
Robert J. Dwyer	Earl Renner	

Korean War Era

Stephen "Red" Awrytis	Erik "Lars' Petersen	Kenny Renak

Cold War

Bob Lauro	Tommy "Doc" Lee

Vietnam Era

Andy Andretta	Tom Krepil	Larry Mendel
Robert Bell, Jr.	Vincent Leibell	Charlie Smyth
John C. Drnek, Jr.	Francis Lyden III	

Between Vietnam & Gulf War

Matt Szpindor	Paul Piazza, Sr.
Michael Nuenar	Randall Mulkins, Sr.

Gulf War to Present

Tommy Gamache	Ricky Medina	Tim Perault
Randall Mulkins	Zachary Mulkins	Justin Shepps

Current Active Members

Andrew Aiken	Arturo Jara	Bret Politi
Alexander Amendoeira	Loretta Kennedy	Philip Porcelli
Terra Avery	Drago Leasa	Conner Raymond
Ken Baker	Tommy Lee	Albert Rossi
John Barretto	Jim Lowe	Andrew Rossi
Freddy Beltran	Dimitrio Martinez	Frank Sabatani
Gene Boo	Dr. Larry A. Maxwell	Harrison Salisbury
Rick Bosser	Frank McDonough	Justin Scheppes
Henry Brunow	Angie McGoorty	John Simpson
Matt Castellano	Ricky Medina	Caleb Franklin Smith III
Edward Centofante	Scott Miller	Paul Smith
Wilson Cajas	Joe Montana	Eileen Smyth
John "Snooky" Covell	Ricky Montana	Adam Stiebeling
Monica Defoe	Vincent Montuoro	Brian Szpindor
Chris Deitz	Randall Mulkins	Justin Szpindor
John Deitz	Zachary Mulkins	Matthew Szpindor
Ann Denholm	Ed O'Connell	Brandy Telesco
James Dipietrantonio	Tim Perault	Sean Terwilliger
Mario Gabrielli	Julian Pettiford	Chris Van Name
Tommy Gamache	Joseph Pignatelli	Raul Vielman
Jesse Greco	Brandon Porcali	Brian Yates
Cody Hickok	Carol Porcali	

Current Active Associate Members

Sue Bouton	Robert Miller
Susan Goldsmith	Debbie Miller

Current Life Members

Andy Andretta	John Covell	Robert Smith, Sr.
George Apap	Robert Cuomo	Robert Smith, Jr.
George Banks	Bob Lauro	James Tence
Willie Boone	Richard Lyden	Stan Vishinski
Louis Chamberlain	Larry Mendel	Lois Ward
Steve Colt	Russell Mulkins, Sr.	Anne Wargo
Lee Conway	James Piazza. Jr.	Curt Wargo

Memorials

Many incredible people faithfully served our department as members and in our Women's Auxiliary. This section contains memorials to some of those awesome individuals sponsored by friends or family.

S. Delvalle "Del" Goldsmith
1906 – 2011

Firefighter, Fire Police & Chaplain

This memorial is sponsored by his family.

In Memory of
Michael K. Semo, Jr.
1941 - 2020

County Legislator & Fire Police

This memorial is sponsored by his children.

William J. Bubenicek
1925 - 1995

Firefighter, Chief
ENCON Captain, Town Justice

This Memorial is Sponsored by His Family

In Memory of
Charles "Charlie" Smyth
1941 - 2019

Firefighter, President & Fire Police

*This memorial is sponsored by his wife and children
All our Love, Eileen, Mike, Tim & Kieran.*

In Memory Of
John Bodor
1941-2016

Life Member, Fire Police Lieutenant

In Memory of
Erik "Lars" Petersen
1922-2016

Firefighter & President

This Memorial is Sponsored by His Family

In Loving Memory of
Diane Vishinski
1949-2020

Lieutenant of the Ambulance, EMT, Trustee

*This Memorial is Sponsored by
Her Husband Stan Vishinski*

In Memory of

Francis R. Brunow

1922-2011

Firefighter & Fire Police

This Memorial is Sponsored by His Son Henry Brunow

In Memory of

Beverly Lauro

1943-2002

Ladies Auxiliary

This Memorial is Sponsored by Her Husband Bob Lauro

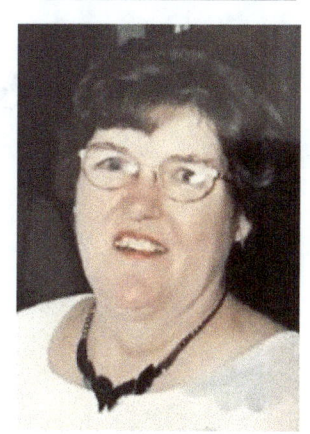

In Memory of

Hollis H. Baker

1917-1986

Firefighter

This Memorial is Sponsored by His Grandson Henry Brunow

Three Angels Who Left Us Too Soon

Cindy Covell   **Paul Piazza, Sr.**   **Diane Vishinski**

This Memorial is Sponsored by John "Snooky" Covell

In Loving Memory Of
Elizabeth McDermott & Fred Buechel

Sponsored by Ann Denholm

Sponsors & Well Wishes

THE ROSSI BROTHERS

ALBERT & ANDREW

SERVING OUR COMMUNITY

"You Light em We Fight em"

EST. 2015

Thank You For Your 100 Years of Faithful Service
From Pastor Larry Maxwell And Your Friends at

Patterson Baptist Church
599 Route 311, Patterson, NY 12563 845-878-4160

Established in 1751 - Serving God & Our Community for 270 Years

---

We Appreciate Your Faithful Service to Our Community For 100 Years
George Apap Painting

Trusted & Dependable Painting Contractors

1278 Route 311, Patterson, NY 12563 - 845-878-3444
info@georgeapapinc.com

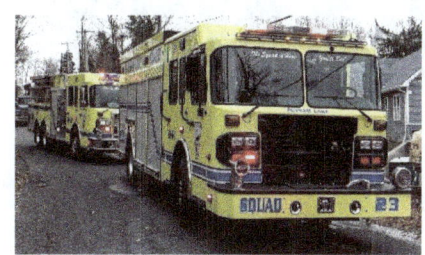

Putnam Lake Fire Department
Est. 1946

Wishing You
A Happy 100 Years!

*It is an Honor Working With You
to Help Protect Our Town*

Proudly Serving
The Patterson
Fire Department
For Three Generations

**Debbie Miller, Loretta Kennedy
Randall Mulkins & Zachary Mulkins**

It Has Been an Honor to Work Together Over the Years
Looking Forward to Working Together for Many More

From Stan Vishinski & The Staff at Stan's Auto Body
3130 Route 22, Patterson, NY 12563   845-878-3500

Honoring
Rosina "Tootsie" Petersen

For 50 Years of Service
in the
Women's Auxiliary
of the Patterson Fire Department

Your Dedicated Service to Our Community is Appreciated!

Happy Centennial

From Your Friends at Clancy Relocation & Logistics
Local & Long-distance Moving and Storage
for your Home or Business since 1921.
Patterson, NY   845-878-3300

Honoring My Wife Lorraine

And All the Wives of Volunteer Fire Fighters
When Their Husbands Are Away at Fires,
Meetings and Funerals

Former Chief and Past President
Robert Bell

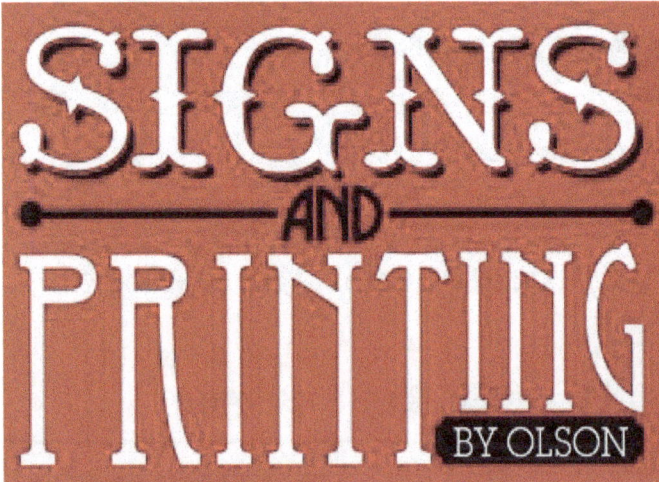

Logo Design • Printing
Signs • Labels & Decals
Banners • Vehicle Graphics
Shirts & Much More!

845-878-2644

2671 Route 22 • Patterson, NY 12563
SignsAndPrintingByOlson
info@SignsAndPrintingByOlson.com

Congratulations on 100 Years

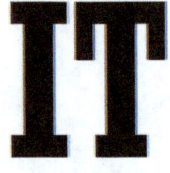

IT Computer Services
**Your Number One Source For
Computers, Upgrades, Repairs
And Web Services**
It is an Honor Serving with You
Arturo_Jara@computerservices.com

Happy 100th Anniversary
from
Brewster Fire Department
Serving Our Community More Than 150 years
It is An Honor Working With You

CONGRATULATIONS!
Patterson Fire Department
100th Year Anniversary
From the Women's Auxiliary

Trudy Mill, *President*　　**Mary Bodor,** *Vice President*
Stacie Spinney, *Secretary*　　**Margaret Kessman,** *Treasurer*
Donna Hazzard, *Chaplain*
Committee: Rosina Petersen, Marlene Fischer,
Bridget Pasko, Ann Montsaano

Thank You for 100 Years of Service to Our Community!
Keep Up the Good Work
Your Friends
at Town Square Pizza Cafe
Route 311, Patterson, Ny 12563

In Recognition of 100 Years of Bravery and Dedicated Service
To the People of the Town of Patterson.
Thank You For All You Have Done and Everything You Continue to Do.
Joe Nickischer, Ex-Chief

Happy 100 Years!
We Appreciate Your Devotion to Our Community

Your Friends at Sauro's
1072 Route 311, Patterson, NY
845-878-3704

Happy 100th Anniversary
From Mario Gabrielli

914-403-7855   mariogab@optonline.net

Claire's
The Perennial Garden Center

210 Haviland Hollow Rd.
845-878-6632

Thank You for 100 Years!

With Gratitude
For Your Faithful Service
From
The Leibell Family

a division of

Thanking the Patterson Fire Department
For 100 Years of Service to Our Town

Christopher Deitz, Captan
and John Deitz, 2nd Asst. Chief
Wish Patterson Fire Department

Happy 100th Anniversary!

It is an Honor for Both of Us to Serve
as Officers and to Be Part of Such
an Historic Event.

The Dry Cleaner

ACME Plaza Route 22
Patterson, NY 845-878-1860

Thank You for Your Service
Your Full-Service Dry Cleaner

CONGRATULTIONS ON YOUR 100 YEARS Of SERVICE

Congratulation for 100 Years Of Service

It Has Been an Honor to Serve With You

Volunteer Fire Department of New Fairfield
302 Route 39, New Fairfield, CT

Happy 100th Anniversary

Keep Up the Good Work

From Your Fellow 1st Responders
at
Kent Volunteer Fire Department

2490 Route 301, Kent, NY 10512

Congratulations On Providing 100 Years of Fire Service to Your Community and Surrounding Mutual Aid Companies

Dover Plains, NY

Randall & Zachary Mulkins

Mom is Very Proud of Both of You

As You Serve Your Community At Patterson Fire Department

I Wish You Well In All the Years Ahead

Members on Our 1927 Hahn

Boosters
These People Helped Sponsor This Book

Thomas & Sue Bouton

Ed & Marie Centofante

John & Chris Deitz

Brandon & Emily Franz

Ron & Debby Franz

Arturo, Maria, Angelica & Natalie Jara

Larry, Becky, Grace, Robert & Violet Maxwell

Joey Nickischer

The Stiebeling Family

Remembering Our Departed Members

This are those who died while members or Life Members who passed.

Edward Anderson	Frank Lyden
Ernest Anderson	Paul C. Maass
Hjalmar Anderson	Thomas MacDougall
Morgan M. Andrey	Thomas E. Malone
Gerald A. Baker	Joseph Naruda
Hollis "Buddy" Baker	Michael Neuner
Henry Ballard	Coleman R. Nichols
Jake Block	David C. Nichols
John Bodor	Patrick L. O'Connell
Howard Booth	Robert Oran
Charles Brazda	Juilus Pahlch, Jr.
Franklin Brown	Horace J. Peck
Francis Brunow	Erik Petersen
Joseph Brunow	George J. Pfahl, Sr.
William J. Bubenicek, Sr.	Julius Pollock
George Buechel	John Radtke
Fred Buechel	Emil F. Renak
Michael C. Burns	Kenneth Renak
William Burns	Andrew Ruthledge
George Burton	Herb Schneck
John Carey	Lewis Schenk
Samuel Carey	Edward Seagrave
Nick H. Comatas	Charles F. Segelken
Rene Connor	Michael K. Semo, Jr.
Cynthia A. Covell	John Sincerbox
William Covell	Theron Smalley
Elbert C. Crosby	Caleb Franklin Smith, Sr.
John Drenner	David C. Smith
William Drnek	Donald B. Smith
Junia W. Dykeman	Emerson Smith
S. Delvalle Goldsmith	Paul Smith
Charles Gronke	Charles Smyth
William Gronke	Stanley Smith
Kenneth A. Hall	Otto Soechtig
Andrew Hampe	Ferris J. Sprague, Sr.
Charles T. Hampe	Albert Starr
Louis D. Harrison	William O. Taylor
Reid F. Haviland	Dr. Albert Towner
Reid L. Haviland	Mortimer B. Townsend
Rev. Horace H. Hillery	Charles H. Van Keuren
Joseph Hinkley	John L. Van Keuren
Frank Huber	Joseph Van Keuren
Albert Hudson	Diane Vishinski
Seth Hudson	Gil Wadle
George Lazar	George Witheridge
Robert E. Lee	R. Fred Wood
Daniel G. Ludington	
Henry S. Ludington	
Francis W. Lyden III	

Remembering Our Departed Women's Auxiliary Members

Linda Alexander
Betty Baker
Nellie Crosby
Catherine Curry
Louise Drenek
Marie Gronke
Mary Gronke
Bessie Hudson
Beverly Lauro
Ann Mulkins
Mary O'Connell

Grethe Petersen
Bodina Scapperotti
Rose Scapperotti
Alice Smith
Ruth Sprague
Nancy Tompkins
Aubrey Wadle
Anna Williams
Olive Wooster
Irene Yerks
Georgiana Zoller

About the Author
Dr. Larry A. Maxwell

The Rev. Dr. Larry A. Maxwell is Chaplain for the Patterson Fire Department as well as an Emergency Medical Technician (EMT) and Fire Police Officer. He is a also a chaplain for the *Putnam Westchester Fire Police Association* and a member of the *New York State Fire Chaplains Association*.

He is an award winning journalist and author of more than 20 books including: *Now and Then Putnam County New York,* written for Putnam County's Bicentennial.

He wrote the book and screenplay, *Sybil Rides the True Story of Sybil Ludington the Female Paul Revere, the Danbury Raid and the Battle of Ridgefield*. Daniel G. Ludington, one of the founding members and past president of the Patterson Fire Department, as well as his father, Henry S. Ludington, our first Chief, are both related to Sybil.

He is a historian and popular conference speaker. He serves as the official Town Historian for the Town of Patterson. That role was also filled by department member Fire Police Lieutenant John Bodor. Dr. Maxwell also served as the Chairman of the *Company of Military Historians* at West Point. He is also a historical advisor for the *History Channel* and for the *New York State Department of Parks and Recreation*.

Dr. Maxwell has served as the Pastor at the *Patterson Baptist Church* for more than 26 years. Some of the founding members of the department, including Junia Dykeman, Chief and the first President of the Patterson Fire Department, were members of that church.

Ud. Puede Ser Un Bombero Voluntario

- Gane un Retiro Mensual
- Obtenga un Credito en su Income Tax y en los Impuestos a la Propiedad
- Fire Dept. Proveera Toda Clase de Equipos

 Esta Ud. Interesado?

Para mas informacion,
Llame o envie un mensaje de Texto
a Arturo Jara C: 845-878-1001

www.ingramcontent.com/pod-product-compliance
Lightning Source LLC
Chambersburg PA
CBHW082106280426
43661CB00089B/892